Illustrated press coverage of the last canonical murder

WHO *WAS* JACK THE RIPPER?

A Collection of
Present-Day Theories
and Observations

Camille
Wolff
GREY HOUSE BOOKS
60 PORTOBELLO ROAD, W11
CRIMINOLOGY
TRUE CRIME
Tel 071 221 0269

Other publications by Grey House Books :

The Story of Mr. George Edalji

WHO *WAS* JACK THE RIPPER?

A Collection of
Present-Day Theories
and Observations

Compiled by Camille Wolff

Grey House Books

1995

First Published in 1995
Reprinted 1995

Grey House Books
60 Portobello Road
London W11 3DL

British Library Cataloguing in Publication Data

A catalogue record for this book is available from the British Library

ISBN 0 9510604 3 0 (Reprint)

Printed and typeset by
Meran Press Ltd.,
Crowhurst Hop Farm,
Bullen Lane,
East Peckham,
Kent, TN12 5LP

CONTENTS

Acknowledgements	
Foreword by Jeremy Beadle	1
Scene Setting	3
Aliffe Andy	5
Anderson David	7
Barber Roger	9
Begg Paul	11
Bloomfield Jeffrey	13
Borowitz Albert	15
Bowden Paul	17
Butler Ivan	19
Chick Edward	21
Evans Stewart	23
Fairclough Melvyn	25
Farson Daniel	27
Feldman Paul	29
Fido Martin	31
Goodman Jonathan	33
Gregg Wilfred	35
Harris Melvin	37
Harrison Paul	39
Harrison Shirley	41
Ives Robert	43
Jones Allan	45
Kendell Colin	47
Luff Ray	49
McLeave Peter	51
McCormick Donald	53

Madden Mark	55
Missen Christopher	57
Nickell Dr. Joe	59
Odell Robin	61
Ogan Jon	63
Oliver Claudia	65
Paley Bruce	67
Rumbelow Donald	69
Shelden Neal	71
Sinclair Iain	73
Smith Christopher	75
Smith Patterson	77
Soothill Prof. Keith	79
Sugden Philip	81
Tapley Brian	83
Tully Jim	85
Underwood Peter	87
Van Eyssen Shirley	89
Waddell Bill	91
Warren Nick	93
Whittington-Egan Molly	95
Whittington-Egan Richard	97
Wilding John	99
Wilkes Roger	101
Wilson Colin	103
Wolf A. P.	105
Wood Simon	107
Wright Stephen	109
Suggested Reading	111

ACKNOWLEDGEMENTS

I would like to express my gratitude to Stewart P. Evans, Keith Skinner and Nick Warren for pointing me in the right direction when attempting to compile a list of contributors to this book. I should also like to thank Lionel Selwyn for reading the texts as they were submitted, Melvin Harris for the use of his scene setting map which was taken from '*The True Face of Jack the Ripper*' and Jonathan Goodman, who was always available, for his very welcome advice and suggestions. Above all, I would like to thank Loretta Lay who co-ordinated this small but complicated book, and managed to keep all 53 contributors happy, even when they wanted to write many hundreds more words than space would permit.

THE LAST MOMENTS OF THE DUKE OF CLARENCE.
A NATION'S CALAMITY.
GRIM DEATH BANISHES THE ANGEL OF HOPE
AND CLAIMS HIS YOUTHFUL VICTIM
SANDRINGHAM HOUSE JANY 14th 1892

IS DEEMING JACK-THE-RIPPER?
JACK
THE RIPPER

FOREWORD

Jeremy Beadle
True-Crime Enthusiast

THIS BOOK IS THE TRUTH, THE WHOLE TRUTH AND NOTHING BUT WHAT THE REAL EXPERTS AND DEVOTED FANS BELIEVE IS THE TRUTH.

Camille Wolff is as hard of hearing as a Whitechapel neighbour but as sharp as Jack's blade. Therefore her keenness for this project is no surprise. Typically and eccentrically this book was inspired by a video. That probably makes it a first.

'The Diary of Jack the Ripper' with a narrative by Shirley Harrison sparked such a storm of controversy, a speculation of Ripperologists gathered together in front of the cameras to discuss it's merits and faults. Was the book a hoax? Was the author duped? Could such an outrageous apotheosis be true?

What stirred Camille was the thought that if a small number of experts can theorise in front of the cameras why couldn't a larger number on the printed page?

Thus this book is unique because it's the first time almost every leading Ripper expert and renowned devotee has been offered and accepted the opportunity to expound their views in a single volume.

Jack baffled, perplexed, tantalised, exasperated. He perpetrated a remorseless series of terrible murders whose bloodcurdling abominations still chill today. Drunk with blood he wrote his infamous letters in red ink because the 'proper stuff.....went thick like glue and I can't use'. The world's first serial murderer went into reverse sex drive and sent hardened police officers reeling in horror. A human butcher with a taste for raw breasts, kidneys, hearts, livers he certainly knew where to get the freshest meat.....around the Commercial Road where he left his trademark but not his name.

He is undoubtedly the best known unknown murderer in the annals of crime. The case is over a century dead yet Jack continues to tease his trackers with new paths to follow, new clues to examine, new suspects to trail. No other single crime has been so exhaustively examined. But still the ghosts of the victims demand justice.

One day we might discover the truth. Perhaps we already know but refuse to believe. Whatever, this anthology offers the most comprehensive catalogue of suspects and solutions ever compiled. Before diving into dedicated tomes I suggest this is the perfect springboard to launch you into the depths of the world's greatest mystery.

Who do I think was Jack the Ripper? I'm not sure I want to know. The hunt is guaranteed to be more exciting than the capture. Pressed I would say look no further than my initials.

Finally a personal note of thanks to Camille Wolff for her endless hospitality and allowing me to spend far more than I should on books I can't live without.

His identity is cloaked in a clinging mist
As mysterious as the twilight he haunted
As sublime as the kiss he gave his victims
As busy as a streetwalker on pay night
As tenacious as a recurring nightmare
As cool as a butcher in a meat fridge
As merciless as the grave
As noiseless as a shadow
As fast as a flash of steel
As keen as a razor
As mad as Satan
As ....

Jeremy Beadle

SCENE SETTING

THE FACTS ABOUT THE EAST END MURDERS AS REPORTED IN THE LONDON TIMES 1888

First Murder	- April 3rd. Victim, Emma Elizabeth Smith. Not reported in The Times.
Second Murder	- April 7th. Victim, Martha Tabram. (aka Turner) Place - Grove Yard Building.
Third Murder	- April 31st. Victim, Mary Ann Nichols. Place - Bucks Row.
Fourth Murder	- Sept. 8th. Victim, Annie Chapman. Place - Hanbury Street.
Fifth Murder	- Sept. 30th. Victim, Elizabeth Stride. Place - Berner Street.
Sixth Murder	- Sept. 30th. Victim, Catherine Eddowes. Place - Mitre Square.
Seventh Murder	- Nov. 9th. Victim, Mary Jane Kelly. Place - Dorset Street. (Millers Ct.)

"The first four victims were women of middle-age. In each case there were abdominal as well as other injuries. In each case the injuries were inflicted after midnight and in places of public resort, where it would appear impossible but that immediate detection would follow the crime.

In the first case a blunt instrument, such as a walking stick was used. In the second case, some of the wounds were thought to have been made by a dagger. But in the third and fourth cases, sharper, similar instruments were used. In both cases the head was nearly severed from the body, and the injuries performed needed anatomical knowledge. In the fourth case, the murder of Annie Chapman, her rings were wrenched from her fingers, and uterus taken from the abdomen. The body had not been dissected but the injuries had been made by someone who had considerable anatomical skill and knowledge. It must have been someone accustomed to the post-mortem room.

The fifth and sixth victims were murdered on September 30th. In the first murder, that of Elizabeth Stride, the body was found in a gateway leading to a factory. The woman only had her throat cut, but little doubt is felt, from the position of the corpse, that the assassin had intended to mutilate it. He seems, however, to have been interrupted by the arrival of a cart, which drew up close to the spot, and it is believed to be possible that he escaped behind the vehicle. The second murder that night (the sixth overall) was that of Catherine Eddowes, in the vicinity of Mitre Square. The constable's beat there is patrolled every fifteen to twenty minutes and within this short space of time the murderer and his victims must have arrived and the crimes committed. Some anatomical skill seems to have been displayed in the way in which the lower part of the body was mutilated, but the ghastly work seems to have been done more rapidly and roughly than in the cases of the women Nichols and Chapman.

The seventh murder, that of Mary Jane Kelly, took place in the early hours of the morning in Spitalfields. All seven murders occurred in the same immediate neighbourhood, and the character of the mutilations leave very little doubt that the murderer in this instance is the same person who has committed the previous ones."

(Extracted from The Fatal Caress ed. by Richard Barker. pub. by Duell, Sloan & Pearce 1947. (1st US edn.))

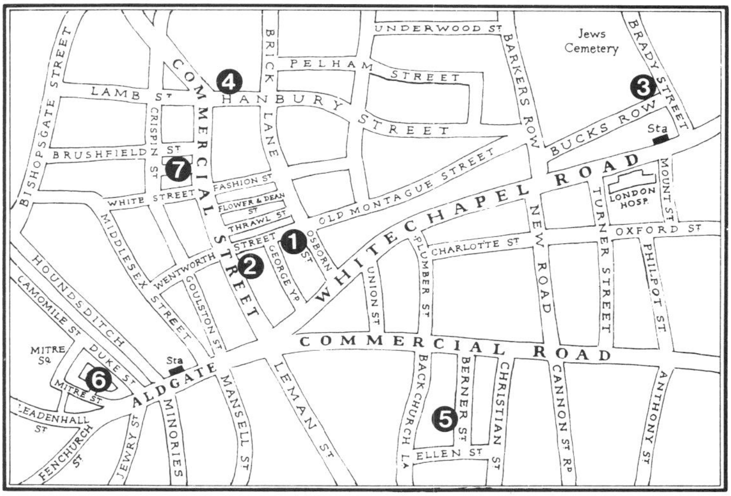

Map of the Whitechapel Murders

1. Emma Smith
2. Martha Turner
3. Mary Ann Nichols
4. Annie Chapman
5. Elizabeth Stride
6. Catherine Eddowes
7. Mary Kelly

Andy Aliffe
TV producer & JTR Enthusiast

RIPPER RAMBLINGS

"On The Day Of Judgement, when all things shall be known, when I and the other generations of Ripperologists ask for Jack the Ripper to step forward and call out his true name, we shall turn and look with blank astonishment at one another as he does and say WHO??", so says Donald Rumbelow in his book The Complete Jack the Ripper.

I have been researching for several years, material for Melvin Harris, concentrating on his suspect, Dr. Roslyn D'Onston-Stephenson. Richard Whittinton-Egan, in his book "A Casebook on Jack the Ripper" first makes mention of a 373 page manuscript written by Bernard O'Donnell entitled "Black Magic and Jack the Ripper" or "This Man Was Jack the Ripper." This manuscript suggests Roslyn D'Onston-Stephenson as a Ripper suspect but has laid unseen for many years, until I recently re-discovered it.

O'Donnell makes an interesting observation of all of the Ripper Killings, that of MOTIVE. Following the categories set out by Miss Tennyson Jesse in her book, "Murder and Its Motives," he quotes; ..."Murder is committed for the following:-

1. Murder for gain.
2. Murder for revenge.
3. Murder for elimination.
4. Murder for jealousy.
5. Murder from conviction.
6. Murder for the lust of killing.

The Whitechapel murders fall into none of these categories. For instance, Jack the Ripper could not hope to GAIN from any of these penniless drabs; there was nothing to AVENGE; there was no need to ELIMINATE them in so far as they stood between him and inheritance or formed the unwanted third party to a triangle; JEALOUSY as we have seen was not the inspiration any more than was the sheer LUST for killing and finally there can be no suggestion that the Ripper murdered from any sense of outraged religious or political CONVICTION." These are the words of Benard O'Donnell and apply to Roslyn D'Onston-Stephenson's motive, that of a Black Magic ritual killing.

There is no shred of evidence so far found to implicate any of the many suspects whose names abound the book shelves of Crime Historians and Ripperologists alike. My own approach to finding a likely suspect would be to apply the Psychological Profiling now being used by some authors, which accounts for research of all known documents of the crimes, the evidence available, behavioural patterns, rage, race, marital status, education, and intelligence. Then based on this established system, SOME of the following attributes can be assumed of JACK the RIPPER.:-

> He was white, in his mid 20's to 30's years of age with average intelligence. Single and a loner, nocturnal. Revisited the scene of the crime and knew the area well. Not accountable to anyone and with a menial job. Erratic behaviour and known to the Police for some minor misdemeanour. Poor personal hygiene. His mental stability would also have been affected by : Coming from a broken home; child abuse; contact with a dominant female; hated and feared women; sexually motivated.

If you then accept that all the Ripper correspondence is a hoax, accept that there WAS some sort of cover-up, and continue to look for papers and documents until a name is found that may have one of the above motives, and some of the profiling factors, you will as I quoted at the beginning, still say .... WHO??

I have contributed original researched material for books by Melvin Harris, several specialist publications, and broadcast on many BBC Local Radio Stations on Ripper related topics.

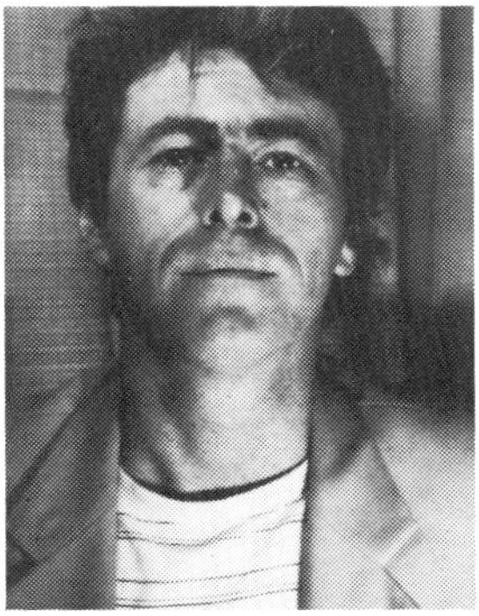

David Anderson
JTR Enthusiast

WHO WAS JACK THE RIPPER?

Of all the suspects so far suggested Montague Druitt still remains the most likely. There is no smoking-gun evidence against him, but there is more than a hint that evidence did once exist. What could this evidence have been?

Sir Melville Macnaghten implies that his 'private information' implicating Druitt came from Druitt's family or friends. Macnaghten has 'no doubt' but that they believed him to have been the Whitechapel Murderer. Could Montague have confessed before his death? and if so to whom? His flight to Chiswick may provide a clue.

Druitt, a keen cricketer, went to Chiswick where his Oxford University friends, the brothers Tuke, owned and ran a private mental asylum. It is most likely that he made his confession to them before taking his own life in the nearby River Thames.

Druitt's mother, Anne, was later cared for at the same asylum. She died there in 1890. Her medical notes describe how she was under the illusion that she was lacking in bodily organs. Druitt's suicide note describes how he felt that he was becoming 'like Mother' - Could this explain his motive for harvesting the organs of his victims?

The fact that Anne Druitt was placed in an asylum just yards from the spot where her beloved son had taken his own life suggests either a great insensitivity toward her feelings, or more likely demonstrates a degree of security in the knowledge that her ramblings would only be known to those who already knew the truth.

In 1970 I discovered in a local newspaper, the now well-known report of Druitt's inquest. There are a number of discrepancies between the first report of the finding of Druitt's body in the river and the evidence given at the inquest. The first report, published before the inquest states that Druitt's identity had been established from papers found upon the body. At the inquest P.C. Moulson testifies that there were no papers or letters found on the body. We do know however that there were some cheques found on Druitt, though after three weeks immersion in water it is questionable as to whether they were readable. It is possible that an identification was made by his friends the Tukes. I suggest also that Druitt's suicide note was written at the asylum in Chiswick. To support this contention consider the phrase 'since Friday.' Had the letter been written on Saturday it is much more likely that he would have used the phrase 'since yesterday.' If this is the case, and since he did not leave Chiswick, his letter must have been found at his destination, together possibly with the other papers, i.e. the cheques and the return-half of his rail ticket.

Macnaghten also tells us that Druitt's own family believed him to have been the killer. Why should they have thought this without good reason?

Macnaghten was a close personal friend of James Monro. Monro himself coincidentally retired to Chiswick where he died in 1924. His neighbour was Charles Tuke, one of the brothers who used to play cricket with Druitt at Oxford. He was the administrator of the asylum.

The killings ceased after Druitt's suicide and the manhunt was scaled down within weeks.

As stated above there is still no direct evidence against Montague Druitt, or indeed anyone else for that matter. Yet Macnaghten, in my opinion, probably comes closer than anyone else when he states that evidence did once exist, and that the truth did indeed once lay at the bottom of the River Thames.

Roger Barber
JTR Enthusiast

DID JACK THE RIPPER COMMIT SUICIDE?

Some researchers suggest that he was incarcerated in an asylum, while others claim that he committed suicide. One thing is certain, he did not lose interest.

Professor Luigi Cancrini of Bologna concluded that the Ripper murders "evinced an explosive crescendo of increasing theatrical violence which would culminate in a complete breakdown."

Colin Wilson says "this destruction of the womb indicated a suicidal tendency."

A likely suspect is a marine stores dealer named Edward Buchan - aged 29 years. He cut his own throat with a knife. He had nearly severed his head from his body. He was the precise age that more than one reliable eye-witness gave for the Ripper; secondly, "he had been strange in his manner for some time past." This could mean that he had been absent for periods with no explanation, perhaps in the early hours. He would have seemed quite normal as far as his everyday work was concerned. Thirdly he was probably a shoemaker at the back of his father's marine stores shop as well as being a sorter in it. The police believed that "Leather Apron" was Jack the Ripper, and that he had been a shoemaker.

It was the womb that fascinated the Ripper. Freudians would infer hatred of the mother, perhaps of younger brothers and sisters stealing the parents' affection etc. Edward Buchan, aged 29, was still living with his father and mother, plus his older sister. He had four brothers and they had all left home.

Jack the Ripper killed two of his victims by cutting their throats with such severity that he cut through the windpipe and back to the spine. The result was that their heads were nearly severed from their necks as happened in Buchan's suicide. With four of the victims, the Ripper tried to remove the reproductive organs. The manner in which the cutting was done suggests he had no medical knowledge and was simply trying to destroy the place he came from. The only victim not to be mutilated in this way was Liz Stride - maybe not because he was disturbed, but because after cutting her neck from behind and turning her over to continue his mutilations, he recognised his victim and panicked. His lust unsatisfied, he went in search of another victim, and found her.

Another fact which makes Edward Buchan the most likely suspect, is the date of his suicide. Monday November 19th 1888 was the day of Mary Kelly's funeral. The people of Poplar would be planning to be on the funeral route. Such attention would enrage the Ripper who was crying out to be noticed - it was also Edward Buchan's birthday. He died in the building in which he had been born. In 29 years he had achieved nothing, and was still tied to his mother. He killed himself on his birthday as a final attempt to break that link - to somehow obliterate his very existence.

So was he Jack the Ripper? The lack of factual evidence suggests that we shall never definitely know who the psychopath was. Psychological evidence alone shows that Edward Buchan is the likeliest candidate to appear.

Paul Begg.
Noted Author on JTR.

WHO WAS JACK THE RIPPER?

Jack the Ripper could have been anybody. Apart from a confession turning up - and the alleged Maybrick Journal has shown with what hostility one of those would be dismissed! - the only real hope of identifying the Ripper is if the police knew who he was. In this context the leading suspects are Druitt, Ostrog, Kosminski, and maybe the person named in the recently 'discovered' Littlechild letter.

That the police - or at least certain senior officers - *did* know the identity of Jack the Ripper is stated by Sir Robert Anderson. In his autobiography he wrote that the murderer was 'a certain low class Polish Jew'. Andeson presented no evidence or proof, but he didn't have to. He was the head of the CID at the time of the murders and might reasonably have expected his word to be accepted.

I began to pursue a hunch that Anderson's unnamed Polish Jew suspect was the same person as called 'Kosminski' by Sir Melville Macnaghten in a memoranda written in 1894. This 'Kosminski' had been committed to, and presumably would have died in an asylum. I didn't find anyone called 'Kosminski' in the asylum records held at the Public Record Office.

However, Martin Fido had made a thorough search of workhouse and asylum records and the only 'Kosminski' he found was in the records of Colney Hatch. There, having been committed by his family in 1892, was an inmate called Aaron Kosminski. But looking at Aaron Kosminski's medical records, Fido concluded that he was not Ripper-like and therefore could not have been Anderson's suspect. Of course, this conclusion depended on Anderson's suspect being the Ripper. If Anderson was wrong, Aaron Kosminski could have been his suspect and could not be dismissed. But I also didn't think the medical records provided sufficient information on which to base such an important conclusion. They were terse, bi-annual reports dealing only with Aaron Kosminski's *physical* health. There was little or no indication as to his mental condition or the precise nature of his delusions. On top of all this, if Aaron Kosminski had spoken German or Yiddish, how many of those charged with his care would have understood what he said? I couldn't be certain, but if Aaron Kosminski had daily declared himself to be Jack the Ripper and described the murders in detail, I doubted whether the existing medical records would have mentioned the fact. I thought Martin Fido had dismissed Aaron Kosminski too hastily.

Anderson gave a few details about his suspect. Aaron Kosminski fitted them all: he was male, Polish, a Jew. He lived in the heart of the district and he had a family. Crucially Anderson also stated that his suspect indulged in 'utterly unmentionable vices...'. This is almost certainly a reference to masturbation, noted as applicable to Aaron Kosminski in his medical papers and in the Macnaghten Memoranda. This, I think, clinches the identification of Anderson's suspect as Aaron Kosminski.

Donald Swanson (who had overall charge of the Ripper investigation) had made some notes in the margins of a personal copy of Anderson's Autobiography. He had glossed Anderson's comments about the Polish Jew suspect. Swanson named that suspect as 'Kosminski'. Swanson confirmed the original hunch that 'Kosminski' was Anderson's suspect and confirmed that 'Kosminski' was Aaron Kosminski.

So, was Aaron Kosminski Anderson's suspect, the man whose guilt Anderson believed was 'a definitely ascertained fact'? I am certain he was, but was Anderson right - was Aaron Kosminski really Jack the Ripper?

Publications:
(on the Ripper)
J the R: The Uncensored Facts.
The Jack the Ripper A to Z (with Keith Skinner & Martin Fido).
Also written about the Ripper for various magazines and journals, including part-works Murder Casebook and Scandal.
TV.
The Secret Identity of Jack the Ripper (USA) - historical adviser.
Jack the Ripper (LWT) - historical adviser, appeared based on book "Uncensored Facts".
Scandal (US) - historical adviser.
Jack the Ripper (Maybrick video) - historical adviser / appeared.
Also spoken on the subject in Britain and Europe.

Jeffrey Bloomfield
American Investigator - Specialist

ON THE DANGER OF WRITING GRAFFITI TOO CLEVERLY

Ever hear of Arthur Lambton? He was a leader in liberalizing British divorce laws, and a founder of "Our Society". In 1931, he wrote ECHOES OF CAUSE CELEBRES. In it he relates the story of the Dalton Murder of 1882. P.C. George Cole was mortally wounded by a burglar he caught. The burglar's chisel was found with the word "rock" on it. Two years later closer examination showed the letters "O" and "R" preceded the word. This helped identify one Thomas Henry Orrock as the murderer. Lambton's friend, Sir Arthur Conan Doyle, admitted to him that this clue was used in the first Sherlock Holmes novel, A STUDY IN SCARLET. Holmes and Watson are examining the body of Enoch J. Drebber. Inspector Lestrade shows a clue. The letters "R", "A", "C", "H", and "E" have been written in blood on a nearby wall. Lestrade believes the killer was writing the name "Rachel". Holmes points out that "rache" is German for "revenge". Later Holmes is proved right.

Researches by various Sherlockians tend to support Lambton's claim. The novel, set in 1881, has many references and inferences to that period. Thomas Carlyle, who died in 1881, is mentioned. Watson, referring to Holmes's violin playing, uses the phrase "trials upon my patience". This may refer to the early Gilbert and Sullivan operettas, culminating in PATIENCE (1881). A second murder victim, Joseph Stangerson, may owe his name to one Urban Napoleon Stanger, who disappeared in 1881. Even Lestrade's reference to a "Miss Rachel" may be based on a notorious swindler, "Madame" Rachel Leverson, who died in prison in 1880.

Doyle must have been proud of this clue with a hidden meaning. It seems likely that he was consulted regarding illustrations. When the noval appeared in BEETON'S CHRISTMAS ANNUAL of 1887, it was illustrated by one D.H. Friston. The writing on the wall was chosen as the frontispiece facing the opening page. It shows Holmes and the others studying the clue.

On 30th September 1888, a prostitute named Catherine Eddowes was murdered. It was the second vicious killing of that night. Near the site of the killing, on a wall on Goulston Street, was written, "The Juwes are the men what will not be blamed for nothing." The killer (we presume) must have thought the public would think the murders were done by a Jew. Only a few would notice that "Juwes" was a term used by the Masons.

Prior to 1888, I have found only one notorious crime where writing was near the victim's body: In the De La Rue Murder of 1845, Thomas Hocker left a *letter* near the victim to mislead the police. Among factual cases none seem to have killers' writing on walls. But not in fictional cases. I do not think it is a coincidence that nine months after Holmes examined "Rache" (and was glaringly shown doing it by his illustrator) the Metropolitan Police were examining "Juwes". Both times the writing is on a wall near a murder scene, and the key word has a cryptic meaning. I feel Jack read A STUDY IN SCARLET, and filed away a trick for future use. Far fetched? Then please tell me of any other actual pre - 1888 murder with a similar cryptic clue written on a wall.

This is the frontispiece from the original edition of
'A Study in Scarlet' - Beeton's Christmas Annual of 1887

Albert Borowitz
American Lawyer and noted author

THE FIRST RIPPER BOOK

Like the course of time itself, the stream of Jack the Ripper publications shows no sign of coming to a stop, but it is possible to identify with precision the earliest Ripper book to come off the presses. This hastily composed little work, whose author wisely decided to remain anonymous, is *The Whitechapel Murders, or Mysteries of the East End.* Published in 1888 after the "double event" but before the butchery of Mary Kelly, *The Whitechapel Murders* sets the pattern for many of its successors by blending fact and fiction.

The narrative begins with the discovery of the body of Martha Tabram, whom the writer lists as the third victim of the Whitechapel murderer, following "Fairy Fay" (December 1887) and Emma Elizabeth Smith (April 1888). The motive of the assassin was bewildering, for the author, like many of the modern commentators, declined to attribute the acts of sexual perversion. Instead, the pamphleteer quotes a journalist's assertion that Jack the Ripper "has hideous malice, deadly cunning, insatiable thirst for blood - all these are marks of the mad homicide". Anticipating Leonard Matters' Dr. Stanley hypothesis, the author cites a theory that "the assassin was some impassioned being who thought he had some injury from the sex and class to avenge". Surely, the killer must be a foreigner, since "brutality in the shape of bloodthirsty hacking was an aggravation for which English society declines to be responsible". The police, however, won the author's support when, for fear of anti-Semitic outrages, they warned the Jews of the East End to stay away from the scene of the Nicholls murder. "To hate the Jew for his religion is bad enough, but to imply his readiness to murder, worse." Equally repellent to the writer of

The Whitechapel Murders was any tendency to discount the horror of the crimes because of the class from which the killer selected his victims.

The Whitechapel Murders reports public criticism of the London police and the resultant organization of vigilance committees. Noting that only the sanitary officials had the authority to inspect lodging houses, the author favoured granting rights of entry to the police and advocated the registration of lodgers and prostitutes. The pamphleteer dramatizes his support for the sorely tested bobbies by introducing a fictional police sleuth, Richard Ryder (Detective Dick), who is hot on the trail of the East End serial killer.

At the end of *The Whitechapel Murders*, the inquest on Catherine Eddowes has been convened and the unknown murderer remains at large:

"The last freak of the lunatic, a scoundrel who signs himself 'Jack the Ripper', is to threaten to begin shortly on Bryant and May's girls, who have been too outspoken as to what they would do if they caught him."

"It is to be heartily hoped that before this human ghoul can find another victim he will be caught, and receive the punishment he so richly merits."

Ripperologists of our day continue to respond loyally to the early pamphleteer's call for the unmasking of Jack. If they have failed in this endeavour, it is not for lack of either ingenuity or ink.

Albert Borowitz Biography

A lawyer residing in Cleveland, Ohio, Albert Borowitz has been described by a critic as "a sleuth upon the crossroads between literature and crime." Borowitz has explored those crossroads through studies of writers, intellectuals and musicians who confronted crime in their own lives. Long before the premiere of *Amadeus,* he wrote a detailed study of the legend of Salieri's murder of Mozart. He has written two book-length crime studies, *The Thurtell-Hunt Murder Case* and *The Bermondsey Horror*. As a mystery novelist, he has created a detective named Paul Prye - who is, like himself, a true-crime aficionado married to an art historian; the first Prye novel is *The Jack the Ripper Walking Tour Murder*.

Paul Bowden
Consultant Forensic Psychiatrist.

WHO WAS JACK THE RIPPER?

I know that this is not the sort of project in which I should be involved. There is no psychiatry of multiple murderers any more than there is one of thieves or arsonists. The behaviours are so rare that it is impossible to draw general conclusions from them; there is no paradigm. The metaphors of mental illnesses do not provide satisfactory answers to 'Who?' questions and in any event to say that a man killed several women because he believed he was John The Baptist raises more questions than it answers.

Neither is putting oneself forward as a psychiatric seer a task I relish. Answering the 'What sort of person are we looking for here?' question is for the naive and the vain. Replies recite the obvious and omit the banal: someone who didn't like his mother or was impotent rather than say, a nurse. Of course the Ripper industry has contributed enormously to the view that what we are seeking is the grotesque. It is not just that multiple murderers usually live next door to someone it is also the fact that we couldn't all be one ourselves.

Psychiatry has proved to have almost nothing to contribute to providing explanations for, or understanding of the multiple murderer. Despite the psychiatrists unrivalled access to these people before trial and after conviction in prisons and maximum security hospitals the literature, both popular and professional is of very poor quality. Books of the Murderers I Knew variety provide either potted case histories or composite and meaningless portraits. Where psychological theories are proposed they are possibility explanations, not telling us why behaviour is inevitable but merely suggesting an association between one event and another. A detailed description of one killer's mind based on say the belief system of a particular psychoanalytical school will have no bearing on understanding another killer. Critics of this view would say that common mechanisms are revealed but in reality what happens is that models become reified: 'as if' becomes 'it is'; the monster-like becomes monstrous.

Multiple murderers are self selected and their characteristics are determined by the single behavioural characteristic which defines the group, their killings. One killer is unlikely to know or understand why he behaves as he does in killing because such knowledge or empathy would preclude the activity itself. Serial killers must be experts in obscuring motives from themselves and even more from those who enquire within them. It is easy to set a number of false trails, ultimately to contradict; to weave elaborate fantasies to those who want to hear such things. A satisfied listener is empowered just as is the one who provides an explanation.

The answer to the question 'Who was Jack The Ripper?' will depend on the needs and expectations of the enquirer. For the policeman it will be an evil genius and hopefully not a humble delivery man; for the crime writer someone who sells books; for the anarchist a member of the royal family and so on. For the psychiatrist it will be someone full of neurotic conflicts, a person who exhibits a complex delusional system including a misidentification syndrome, instructing and threatening auditory hallucinations and a complete lack of insight. Such people are rarely met and almost never in the pages of a Who's Who? of serial killers. Perhaps it is the unknowability of Jack which allows for the projection of a range of identities whose nature and characteristics depend on the hang-ups of the person who thinks he has caught his man?

Paul Bowden is a consultant forensic psychiatrist. He has examined more than a thousand killers.

Ivan Butler
Noted author including "Murderers' London & England"

THE FINAL FINAL SOLUTION

The identity of Jack the Ripper need remain a mystery no longer to anyone who studies one of the most famous and edifying of all Diaries - that of Mr Charles Pooter, of The Laurels, Holloway, a man with the utmost regard for respectability, on the surface.

THE BACKGROUND: Mr Pooter worked in the City, with easy access to (and knowledge of) the East End. His newly bought "nice six-roomed residence" had a "nice little back garden" running down to the railway. His "dear wife Carrie" was a heavy sleeper, unlikely to be disturbed by any midnight activities her husband might pursue.

THE COINCIDENCES (too many, surely to be accurately regarded as such): The first entry in the Diary is for April 3rd (1888), the day after (on Easter Monday) Emma Smith was murdered in Spitalfields.

On April 29th Mr Pooter "experienced the greatest fright I have ever received in the whole of my life" when, getting out of a hot bath he found himself covered from head to foot in blood - a hallucination dreadful enough to unbalance the steadiest mind. He had, in fact, forgotten that he had painted the entire bath red - an odd thing to do in any circumstances. (He also painted a towel-horse, a washstand, a coal-scuttle, the backs of his Shakespeare volumes, a pair of old boots, his friend's walking-stick - a suspiciously strange obsession with the colour of blood.)

On August 6th (Bank Holiday) he was horrified to learn that his dear son, Lupin, had been sacked (apparently with glee rather than remorse) from the job in a bank that he had painstakingly found for him. On August 7th Martha Turner was found stabbed to death in George Yard Buildings.

On October 30th he writes that four or five weeks had been "wilfully torn" (ripped?) from his Diary by an "unknown hand". During that very period occurred the murders of *four* Ripper victims! "Unknown"? It is surely clear that he had had a sudden realisation of how dangerous it was to record - or even hint at - his sinister activities, and decided that his Diary must be treated as a cover-up rather than a revelation. Driven to distraction by worry over the unreliable Lupin, and maddened by such infuriating mysteries as the discovery of a large brick flung into his beloved geraniums, he had clearly allowed his secret blood-lust to erupt into the orgy of those weeks of horror.

A few days later, to his father's utter dismay, Lupin announced his engagement ("without consulting us") to Daisy Mutlar, a woman eight years older than himself. On November 8th (a fatal date) Miss Mutlar's younger brother, a "gawky youth" and a keen member of a theatrical group known as the Holloway Comedians (of which Mr Pooter "strongly disapproved") lured the easily led Lupin out with him until "well after midnight". Mr Pooter obviously followed them (to what dreadful dens of vice we can only imagine) and finally, in a fury of frenzy and despair, committed his climactic murder - that of Mary Jane Kelly in Miller's Court.

Thereafter, his lust for blood sated (and perhaps a final blow struck for respectability) he learnt to live with his troubles, and even found a measure of peace.

So there it is. If there is one certainty among all the shifting mysteries of Jack the Ripper it is that he was an *unnoticeable* man rather than the dark, looming figure of legend. He was in fact a Nobody.

A fuller account of the case against Mr Pooter is to be found in my essay "Jack the Ripper Unmasked", first published in the Literary Review, and later included (as "Charles the Ripper") in Jonathan Goodman's very suitably entitled *Masterpieces of Murder*.

Other real-life crime books:
Murderers' London (Robert Hale)
Murderers' England (Robert Hale)
The Trials of Brian Donald Hume (David & Charles)
and the following essays:
"Death of a Countess" (in Jonathan Goodman's *The Railway Murders*)
"A Slaying on Saint Valentine's Day" (in Jonathan Goodman's *The Supernatural Murders*)

E.W.G. Chick
Canadian JTR Theorist

A QUESTION OF IDENTITY AND MOTIVE

Whitechapel 1888. A miserable area in the East-End of London, described contemporaneously as the evil quarter mile, and with just cause. Brutal murders, particularly of women were common-place, but none captured the horror of the five murdered and horribly mutilated women attributed to the killer known as Jack the Ripper. Newspapers of the day sensationalised every last detail. This was especially so with the fifth victim Marie (Mary) Jeannette Kelly, the youngest and most attractive of all the murdered women, whose savagely mutilated body was found in bed in her rented room at Miller Court, Dorset Street, on Lord Mayor's day November 9, 1888.

The identity of the murderer and the motive for the killings occurring over a ten week period has been a subject of discussion and speculation from that time, so aptly named by Cullen as the Autumn of Terror.

The suspects. Many and of varied backgrounds but of those questioned or arrested by the Police authorities, main interest has centred on one Jack Pizer known as Leather Apron, Joseph Barnett who had been living with Mary Kelly, and Tom Cutbush, nephew of a retired Scotland Yard Executive Superintendent. In recent years favoured suspects have been Montague Druitt, Barrister, Aaron Kosminski, a Polish barber, and Michael Ostrog, a Russian Doctor and given credibility having been named in papers belonging to Sir Melville Macnaghten, appointed to succeed Police Commissioner Sir Charles Warren.

Also finding some support as viable suspects, are Prince Albert, Duke of Clarence, heir Presumptive to the throne and known as Prince Eddy, Sir

William Gull, Physician in Ordinary to Queen Victoria, and J.K. Stephen, Tutor to the Prince.

Sparking interest anew has been the discovery of a diary allegedly written by a Liverpool businessman, James Maybrick and claiming to have been Jack. Mrs. Maybrick was charged in 1889 with his murder. She was tried and found guilty by Mr. Justice Stephen, father of J.K.

Who was Jack the Ripper? Was he the highest in the land, a barrister, or an asylum inmate, a tutor with reputedly homosexual yearnings for the Prince? Or could it be a person actually close to one or all of the victims? Known to them and trusted. Police statistics reveal quite clearly that in the majority of murder cases, the killer is known to the victim, and is either a member of the family, a friend, a neighbour or at least an acquaintance.

Of the suspects identified, one person stands alone as fitting the statistical profile, namely Joseph Barnett who had been living with Mary Kelly for several months.

Barnett, an unemployed fish porter, was infatuated with Kelly, but arguments were frequent, primarily over her excessive drinking, and her resorting to prostitution, and especially abhorrent to Barnett, her bringing home other prostitutes to share her bed.

The effect on Barnett would be traumatic, an affront to his masculinity and increasingly he would likely have developed a hatred of prostitutes leading to an obsession. It is known that all murder victims attributed to Jack the Ripper were acquainted with Kelly and Barnett. Possibly, to satisfy his increasing hatred of prostitutes and to shock Kelly into changing her ways, it would seem to Barnett, in his emotional frame of mind, that to kill those who Kelly knew could produce a change in her behaviour. Perhaps only one murder was initially intended, but as Kelly continued to work the streets and brought home prostitutes so the murders continued. Finally in a brooding fit of rage his madness culminated in the horrific murder and terrible mutilation of Kelly herself. The trigger could well have been her supposed pregnancy, given his state of mind and her occupation.

Who was Jack the Ripper? His identity was not known in 1888 and it is unlikely we shall now ever discover the truth. The type of person Barnett was is not dissimilar to serial killers caught to date.

Stewart P. Evans
Serving police officer/JTR Enthusiasist/contributory author

THE LITTLECHILD LETTER

One of the few bonuses of the centenary "madness" was the meeting of the three researchers/authors, Begg, Fido and Skinner who were to usher in a new era of informed and meticulously researched work on the case. They proved there was still much to be added, and identified the numerous corrigendum that existed. "The Jack the Ripper A to Z" appeared. My interest was rekindled. Was the identity of the unknown Victorian killer forever to remain a mystery? They indicated perhaps not.

The old hope of all Ripper aficionados that somewhere there may be a long-lost dusty document, possibly identifying the Ripper, may not be such a pipe-dream after all. The emergence over the years of such items as the Macnaghten memoranda, the Swanson marginalia and the return of the previously lost original "Dear Boss" letter and Dr. Thomas Bond's report on the Kelly autopsy, in 1988, indicated that there was indeed material "out there" waiting to be found.

The revelation that the "journal" of "Jack the Ripper" had been found in 1991 seemed too good to be true. It is a huge leap from finding "lost" case papers to what amounts to a written confession. A leap, I fear, that is just too great. The most objective of the experts agreed, it was a modern hoax. Those of a more cautious character claimed it was very clever and required further research in an effort to positively disprove it. The book and video appeared. There were pros also - the new detailed research was disclosing still more facts on the case. In July 1992 surgeon Nick Warren had launched his pioneering forum for all Ripper enthusiasts, Ripperana. This revealed a previously hidden body of dedicated researchers and budding authors. Some of the old but unresearched suspects were fleshed out and, in some cases, disposed of altogether as suspects.

It was into this arena that I found myself thrust when, in February 1993, I entered the reckoning in an unexpected way. As a long-time collector of crime ephemera, my name was already quite well known amongst dealers, collectors and writers. Thus it was, at that time, I received a telephone call from a noted but now retired dealer. "Would you like to buy some Jack the Ripper letters?" the voice asked, and he went on to explain that he had some letters written in the early 1900's to the writer George R. Sims. It was the remains of Sims' collection. Sims was a contemporary writer on the Whitechapel Murders. I received a packet containing four letters and two press cuttings. One letter was from Chief Inspector John George Littlechild who was at the head of Monro's Secret Department, or Special Branch at Scotland Yard in 1888. He did not retire until 1893 and was in a position of great importance at the Yard throughout the investigation of the Ripper slayings.

On the first page of this letter Littlechild names a strong contemporary police suspect, an American, whose name I had not seen in any of the books. As a suspect Littlechild rated him "a very likely one". On the same page Littlechild identifies two pressmen who were "generally believed at the Yard" to be responsible for the name "Jack the Ripper", the originators of the "Dear Boss" correspondence. Also contained in the letter was important information on the investigation into the cases of Oscar Wilde and Harry Thaw, the wealthy American murderer. At the end of the letter Littlechild adds, by hand, "I knew Major Griffiths for many years. He got his information from Anderson who only 'Thought he knew'". The significance of this letter was great, it would open up new avenues of research and explain some aspects with regard to the case that had previously been mystifying.

The April 1993 issue of Ripperana carried the first public disclosure of my find. I drove to Malvern where I saw the long-time Ripper expert and old friend, Richard Whittington-Egan. He became the first to see the Littlechild letter and was intrigued by its revelations. He encouraged me to progress with research and Keith Skinner began work on it. In a very short time Keith had identified the suspect historically and stated "He's looking good." Paul Begg and Martin Fido were also involved and work is continuing. It is featured in the new and completely revised "Jack the Ripper A to Z".

Stewart P. Evans is a serving police officer with 25 years service and has appeared on television and radio in interviews regarding the Ripper mystery. He also appears, in a contributory role, in Fido and Skinner's book "The Peasenhall Murder", and in the new edition of the "Jack the Ripper A to Z" by Begg, Fido and Skinner. He contributes occasional articles to Ripperana.

Melvyn Fairclough
JTR Author

WHO WAS JACK THE RIPPER?

Like Stephen Knight's book, 'Jack the Ripper: The Final Solution', my own book, 'The Ripper and The Royals', published by Duckworth in 1991, was based on information from Joseph Sickert who, in turn, got the story from the celebrated English Impressionist, Walter Sickert, whom Joseph claims was his father. He said that he gave Knight half the story only and that what he told me was the conclusion to it. The story, now well known, was that the Ripper's victims were killed to cover up an affair between the Duke of Clarence and a Roman Catholic commoner, Annie Crook, who was Joseph's grandmother.

Since publication of my book I have been one of several who have helped Paul Feldman in his research into the background of the diary, signed Jack the Ripper, which surfaced in Liverpool recently.

My belief now is that this diary is genuine and was written by James Maybrick, a Lancashire cotton merchant whose wife Florence was imprisoned for his murder, by poisoning, in 1889. The consensus among crime historians is that Florence was innocent.

It has been said by some that the diary is a modern forgery. It seems to me that these 'Ripper' authors have been too keen to protect their own unproven theories. They should have the courage to look at this diary more objectively than they have hitherto done. The diary is owned by Anne Barrett (née Graham), who was given it by her father William Graham, who claims that Florence Maybrick was his grandmother, and that he was given the diary in 1950. If the diary is a modern forgery the cynics *must* accept the following:

That either Anne or her father are the forgers and are capable of fooling ink and paper experts and have knowledge of ESDA tests and ion migration; that they are in collusion with the Johnsons (who own the Maybrick watch containing the initials of the Ripper's victims). They must also have known more about James Maybrick and Jack the Ripper than any historian or previous author, as well as a history of Victorian word usage. They would also have needed a knowledge of the psychopathology of serial killers and a deep understanding of the effects of arsenic and strychnine. The detractors would also have to admit that it is a lucky coincidence that Florence Maybrick called herself Mrs Graham when she left prison; that it was extremely lucky for the forgers that the initials FM were on the wall of Kelly's room; that it was a mere coincidence that the initials JM were on an envelope found at Chapman's murder site and that the first two and last two letters of James Maybrick's name spell Jack!

What is particularly interesting from a personal viewpoint, is that Joseph Sickert's tale *echoes* much of the Maybrick story. In both, for example, a woman was imprisoned for a crime she did not commit. Also J.K. Stephen was the son of Florence Maybrick's trial judge, James Fitzjames Stephen; Sir William Gull was J.K. Stephen's doctor and that of Lord Randolph Churchill's wife, Jennie.

Joseph Sickert is partially deaf. His mother, Annie Crook's daughter Alice, who also told him many details of his story, was 'stone deaf', according to work house records. I believe that down the last century, in a series of 'Chinese whispers', the true story — that of James and Florence Maybrick, and many of the names of those directly or indirectly involved — was inadvertently distorted.

Allan Jones, an amateur Ripperologist with an impeccable eye for detail, has discovered, living in a small section of Cardiff in the 1880s and 90s, all the names in Joseph's story. Included is that of Jim Driscoll, a famous boxer and friend of Walter Sickert and Joseph's stepfather, William Gorman. Driscoll, it now seems, *was* related to Mary Kelly, and there is evidence to suggest that Kelly was not the one murdered in her room — just as Joseph told me and as I wrote in the last chapter of my 'book.' Could it be that Joseph is the grandson of Mary Kelly and not Annie Crook? Has he got the story the wrong way round? Was Kelly the Catholic connection? Finding out will be the next project.

Melvyn Fairclough

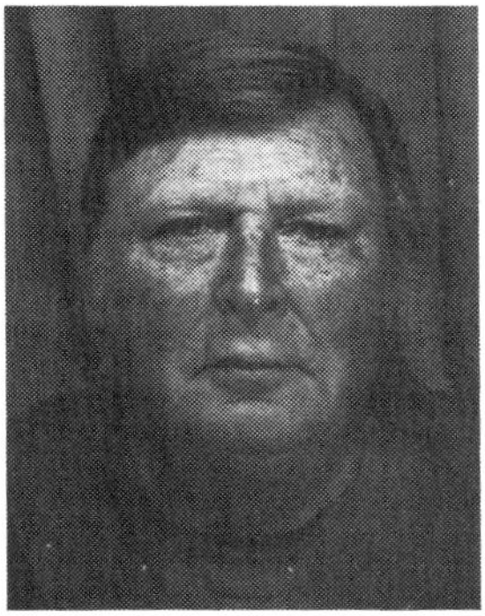

Daniel Farson
Noted JTR author

THE CASE AGAINST MONTAGUE JOHN DRUITT

Jack the Ripper, disguised or otherwise, was probably not particularly remarkable, and must have mingled with hundreds of people in the East End. The commercial traveller, Lawende, who saw Catherine Eddowes talking to a man ten minutes before she was killed, describes him as '30 years old, 5' 9" in height, with a small fair moustache'. Druitt was thirty-one, and although it is hard to judge from the photograph just how dark or fair he was, there is the beginning of a small moustache.

Much has been made of the suggestion that the Ripper was ambidextrous. The Curator at Winchester College said: "MJD's sporting career should give us a clue to his use of his hands. To be as good as he was at Fives, he must at least have had a lot of strength in both arms and wrists".

The police photographs convey an instant impression of how the murderer ripped his victims apart. Also the extra strength in both arms conveys a further impression of the way Druitt worked, stabbing fiercely with both hands.

Perhaps Martha Turner really was a Ripper victim. Dr. Keleene was convinced that two weapons had been used - but why? The obvious deduction was that the murderer used a long bladed knife and possibly a surgical instrument when he killed Martha Turner.

Pathologist, Dr. Keith Simpson told me that if the Ripper had been a doctor, his lust for cutting up bodies would have been satisfied by his work, or he would have been so extreme that his colleagues would have noticed it.

But I believe that he had some basic medical or surgical knowledge - Druitt's father, uncle and cousin Lionel were all doctors and Druitt might have attended post-mortems. The police suspected the Ripper used a post-mortem knife.

I am certain that the Ripper had access to some private rooms near the scene of the murders. This would explain why the murders were committed within such a small radius, and how he managed to escape.

In 1959 I saw Sir Melville Macnaghten's private notes where he identified Montague John Druitt as the leading police suspect. William Druitt, the elder brother, believed that Montague was the Ripper. Several leading representatives of the police and Home Office made separate statements claiming the Ripper was found in the Thames at the end of December 1888; undeniably this man was Druitt. A link is established between Druitt and the East End with the existence of Dr. Lionel Druitt's surgery in the Minories as early as 1879. The Minories was referred to in one of the letters from the Ripper and lies within a few minutes walk of the various murders. A letter written by Dr. Lionel Druitt was printed by a Mr. Fell of Dandenong in Australia in 1890. The document was called 'The East End Murderer - I knew him'. Dr. Lionel Druitt did practice there, and Mr. Fell existed. Montague Druitt was ambidextrous; he may well have had surgical knowledge; he feared he was going insane, like his mother; above all, his brother and the police must have been in possession of some proof to believe that Montague Druitt was the Ripper.

I believe that as he walked into the cold void of dawn, satiated yet empty, his brain trembled for a moment and he realised what he had done. He revealed this knowledge in papers left for his brother William, and then took his own appalled and appalling life.

Reproduced with the author's permission from 'Jack the Ripper', pub. by Michael Joseph in 1972.

Paul Feldman
Executive Producer of the video of 'The Diary of Jack the Ripper'

WHO WAS JACK THE RIPPER?

The publisher's introduction to 'The Diary of Jack the Ripper' is included here for the benefit of the general public who are not necessarily Ripper experts.

'The owner of the Diary is Michael Barrett, an ordinary working man from Liverpool. Mr Barrett told us that a friend, Tony Devereux, gave the Diary to him in 1991 - Devereux died a few months later without revealing how he came by it. We, therefore, do not yet know where the Diary came from'.

Much of the work our research team undertook centred around discovering the true provenance of the Diary. Our belief in the Diary was due, in the main, to the fact that no expert scientific or historical could disprove the document. Psychologists and graphologists have been unanimous in their belief that this document has been written by a very sick and disturbed individual. The Diary has been examined by eminent scientists of the world. It passed all ink and paper tests carried out on it and there was not one scientist who would say that the ink and paper were inconsistent with Victorian age. I have challenged those who say that anyone can go out and buy a bottle of Victorian ink. So far they have been unable to produce the goods. The Diary also passed the ESDA test. American scientists carried out an ION migration test which showed the Diary to be written, somewhere between 1909 and 1931, not too far away from the 1889 when it needed to be written.

The gold watch, which has recently turned up in the ownership of the Johnson brothers, was put through the most testing of scientific analysis, by

Dr Wilde of Bristol University and Dr Turgoose of UMIST and found to be "many tens of years old".

Are the cynics really asking us to believe that Michael Barrett has an understanding of all these scientific elements? That he has such knowledge of both Maybrick's life and the Jack the Ripper crimes that not one expert in the entire country can trip him? That he also understands the psychopathology of a serial killer? That his knowledge of Victorian language is first rate?

On the face of it the most damming piece of evidence against the Diary appeared to be the handwriting. It was compared to what appeared to be the Will of James Maybrick currently resting at Somerset House. But evidence shows (MacDougall 1891 and Liverpool Echo 30.7.1889) that the original Will of James Maybrick had an Affidavit of Due Execution attached to it. Somerset House have since told us that the Will that is currently with them "did not have an Affidavit of Due Execution attached to it and would not have needed one!"

In 1904, when Florence Maybrick left prison, (having been found guilty of the murder of her husband in 1889) we learnt that she called herself 'Mrs Graham'. This is the maiden name of Michael Barrett 's wife Anne. She allowed me to interview her father who explained that his father was the illegitimate child of Florence Maybrick, conceived when she was 15 or 16. Florence Maybrick was most certainly in the country at the time that the baby was born.When she died in 1941, in Conneticut, her address book was found with all the 'G's' torn out. Interestingly, a photograph of Florence Maybrick in her older age, and a photograph of William Graham's father show a marked similarity between them.

There is not one single piece of evidence that has been produced against this Diary that cannot be answered. The theory of a forgery involving individuals with the expertise abilities that would be required is simply preposterous. Of course, the Diary is real and there is a growing belief in the media that this is the case. Our research team have uncovered families of illegitimate Maybrick's. These revelations have not surprised them whatsoever and most of them believe that this has always been known within the family. Time will reveal all.

Martin Fido
Crime Historian

THE RIPPER KILLINGS

The Ripper killings were self evidently the work of a sadistic sexual maniac. Any responsible attempt to identify him must rest on evidence from the period (not modern attempts to fit data to a sudden new suspect). The historian's questions must be:

1. Did anyone from the time say he or she knew the killer's identity?
2. Was he/she in a position to know?
3. Does his/her account match the demonstrable facts of the case (as given, e.g., in sworn inquest testimony)?
4. Was he/she a reliable person with a good record for truth and accuracy?

Only *one* person fits all the above criteria: Robert Anderson. Unfortunately, his fourfold repeated claim that the Ripper was identified gives very limited details: a poor Polish Jew from Whitechapel, identified , only after the suspect was certified insane, by a Jewish witness who was the sole person ever to have had a good sight of the murderer. Nevertheless, if Anderson's were the sole testimony we had on this line of enquiry, a search of asylum records around London at the time leaves as the undoubted prime suspect "David Cohen", a poor immigrant Jew from Whitechapel placed in the Workhouse Infirmary by the Metropolitan Police four weeks after the last murder, and transferred to Colney Hatch two weeks later, where he died the following year. His records indicate some doubt about his actual name and address.

In support of Anderson, however, we have the Macnaghten Memoranda and Swanson Marginalia, both naming the alternative suspect

(Aaron) Kosminski. Neither claimed Anderson's certainty that the Ripper had been identified, and Macnaghten definitely preferred another suspect. Both include demonstrable error in their reporting, though both men were essentially truthful.

Since Kosminski was not certified until 1891 and his records show no serious trace of violence and no violent fantasy whatever, he seems most unlikely to be either Anderson's suspect or the Ripper. Indeed, were he Anderson's suspect, Anderson would be seriously discredited as a detective, accepting a single eye-witness's unique identification of a stranger two years after the sighting. I concluded, before the Swanson Marginalia were known to exist, that somehow Kosminski had been confused with Cohen who was the real suspect and probable Ripper.

When the Swanson marginalia emerged, it proved that he said Kosminski was under restraint when incarcerated and died shortly after transfer to Colney Hatch. Both points were untrue - the second extravagantly so, since Kosminski was still alive when he wrote it 19 years after the transfer. Both points, however, apply to Cohen, immensely increasing the probability that my postulation that the two men had been confused with each other was correct.

I suggest tentatively that the reason for the confusion was that the Metropolitan Police covertly used the City Police witness Joseph Lawende to identify Cohen, while the City were covertly watching Kosminski on Metropolitan territory. Since both men were the same age and went into the same asylum (separately) the Met. subsequently assumed the City had been watching their man, and erroneously accepted details of Kosminski which had been ascertained by the City to resolve their own uncertainties about their (by now deceased) suspect.

The mundanity of this local suspect further strengthens the case.

CONTRIBUTIONS TO RIPPER LITERATURE

The Crimes, Detection and Death of Jack the Ripper, Weindenfeld and Nicolson, London, 1987; revised pbk 1989; repr Orion, London, 1994; repr with new Introduction, Barnes & Noble, NY 1994.

The Jack the Ripper A to Z (with Paul Begg and Keith Skinner), Headline, London, 1991; revised pbk, 1992; revised and updated, 1994.

Contributions to *Real Crime Book Digest* (Chicago).

Jonathan Goodman
Noted True-Crime author

ROUND THE BEND?

In a book called *'Who He?'* (1984), which the publishers Buchan and Enright subtitled 'Goodman's Dictionary of the Unknown Famous', I included a spoof entry for the "real" Jack the Ripper:

'Harpick, Peter J.

A transvestite sculptor, innovative in his use of Plasticine, whose mother Adascha Harpick, nee Schmidt, was a keen cricketer (collections of sports statistics, though not 'Wisden', record that she scored a half-century on behalf of a Women of Kent XI during a friendly match with the Ladies of South Kensington at Fontwell Park in 1860) and whose father Wally is said to have been descended from the Romanovs by way of a Brighton peer. In early manhood, after studying under Dr. Wilhelm Bunbury at the Chorlton-cum-Hardy Polytechnic, Harpick developed an obsession that his mother was a surrogate, standing in, as it were, for a woman of Whitechapel's unfortunate class who had actually borne him. In the autumn of 1888, he determined to put an end to all prostitutes in that area, and being methodical, started off with those who were unfortunate enough to have an "a" in their names. After doing away with a half a dozen, between times writing provocatively to the press, signing the messages with an anagram of his name, he became bored with the idea, and retired to Southeast London, where he died in obscurity soon after publishing his monumental work, 'Statues to be Observed in Penge and Its Environs: a Rambler's Guide' (1903), which was dedicated to "my only true begetter, Mr. W.H." (his late father, of course).'

I meant that to poke fun at the "Hunt the Ripper" game: I assumed that all readers would understand that the name of my "candidate" was an anagram of the alias, that the potted biography was a fiction - therefore, I was surprised to receive a letter from a Ripperologist requesting further information about Peter J. Harpick, and I remain astonished that a dozen other people subsequently wrote me similar letters. I must say, I found it rather hard to compose polite replies. The fact that I, not intending to fool a single reader, fooled a number of them just goes to show how easy it is for Ripper writers who aim to deceive readers into accepting their particular candidates to achieve partial success: the simple trick is to put forward a few biographical truths that do not conflict with the notion that the candidate fills the bill, add some assumptions in the guise of truths, and omit—or think up a way of discounting—proof that the theory is nutty.

Early in 1988, the Ripper Centenary Year, the *Daily Telegraph* gave considerable publicity to a new hair-brained assertion that Jack had been identified. The paper published a letter of mine to the editor, pointing out objections to the theory and ending: "Let us agree that Jack the Ripper was Peter J. Harpick and leave him at that." And again I received tell-us-more-about-Harpick mail. Later in the year, when the Centenary Celebrations were in full swing, I wrote "Whitechapel Blues", which was first published in the monthly *True Detective*:

A hundred years since Ripping Jack—
Forgive me if I don't look back;
I'm tired of Clarence, Chapman, Druitt—
None of them had the nous to do it .
Another thing: we can't be sure
If there was one Jack, two, or more:
Copy-cat killings have been known
To be ascribed to one alone.
There's all the talk of "Jill" as well—
Lily Langtry, Ethel M. Dell:
Maybe it was a fatal femme,
But frankly, I don't give a damn.
So far as I'm concerned, the rippin'
May all have been done by Dr. Crippen.
I know he wasn't even here; he
Was in the States. It's just a theory—
Along the lines of those I've heard
From Ripper buffs, and quite as absurd.
There you observe my boredom's root:
Hunt the Ripper is a trivialized pursuit. ***

*** From a revised edition of *Bloody Versicles: The Rhymes of Crime* (Kent State University Press, USA 1993)

Wilfred Gregg
True Crime Author

JACK WHO?

When the Ripper was prowling the mean streets of Victorian Whitechapel, he could never have imagined that his bloody depredations would years later introduce a new word: "Ripperology". A Ripper mythology has built up unequalled by other unsolved serial killings. "Jack the Stripper" and the "Zodiac Killer" although not yet having the Ripper's advantage of age are probably just as interesting but neither has engendered legends. Those two murderers may never achieve the Ripper's fame as fans of the former are unlikely to want to be known as "Stripperologists" while "Zodiacology" does not have quite the right ring about it.

Ripperologists have given lengthy and often over earnest consideration to many suspects, few of whom deserve to be considered. It's clear that some of the theorists have picked a suspect first and then tailored the "evidence" to fit their nominee. Many of the suspects have been convicted of other murders; the suspects have ranged over all social classes with a pre-disposition towards the middle and upper ones.

The category of "other-case murderers" includes Neill Cream (apparently spirited from a Chicago prison and across the Atlantic without benefit of Concorde; the theory stems from alleged remarks by the doctor a split-second before he was hanged at Newgate); poisoner George Chapman, alias Klosowski; Frederick Bailey Deeming, simply because of another doubtful confession prior to execution (in Australia); the Scottish wife-murderer William Henry Bury and the Broadmoor escapee James Kelly.

Artisan's are represented by a Jewish slaughterman; Mary Kelly's alleged lover, Joseph Barnett; John Pizer alias "Leather Apron" and the coach driver John Netley who has been put forward as the driver for the Ripper, (to whom he presumably respectfully touched his forelock as he helped him off the coach and passed him the knife). A suspect with an East End connection was the paranoid stabber Thomas Cutbush. Foreigners are represented by Aaron Kosminski, Michael Ostrog, Dr. Alexander Pedachenko, Nicolai Wassili and Manuel Cruz Xavier. Even the gentle sex has its nominees with a midwife or transvestite Jill the Ripper and Olga Tchkersoff, who sounds as if she would have been more at home in a Russian anarchist circle than in Mitre Square.

In the middle and upper classes, one finds the self-styled Roslyn D'Onston alias Stephenson; lawyer/cricketer Montague Druitt; the eminent physician Sir William Gull; surgeon's son John Sanders; the painter Walter Sickert; Leonard Matters' "Dr. Stanley"; tutor J.K. Stephen; Dr. William Wynn Westcott, and more recently "James the Ripper" Maybrick.

Even Royals have been named as suspects: most spectacularly Queen Victoria's son the Duke of Clarence no less, (another who would have had to overcome time and distance by being in two places at the same time). Thankfully, the Queen had departed to Eternal Majesty at the time this theory was propounded; certainly she would "not have been amused" by the suggestion nor by the lip-smacking publicity given to his sexual proclivities.

I have mentioned only comparatively few of the suspects who have been put up by Ripperologists. It seems to me that Jack's identity was best summed up by Joe Gaute: that, on Judgement Day Ripperologists will exclaim "Who" when Jack rears his perhaps ugly head and claims the title from the umpteenth unwitting impostor.

Wilfred Gregg co-wrote: The Encyclopaedia of Serial Killers and The Encyclopaedia of Mass Murder.

Melvin Harris
Noted JTR author

WHO WAS JACK THE RIPPER?

Since 1888 the public has been duped unmercifully by Ripper 'solutions' based on hoaxes, fantasies or outright fiction. But the truth is that out of all the mass of documents and newspaper reports, only four authentic candidates have ever emerged, and three of these were simply Macnaghten's homicidal maniacs.

My first verdict on the Whitechapel mystery was an open one. Since none of the contending theories stood up to close scrutiny, the killer was sure to be someone unknown, someone unsuspected. Later, my interest in the FBI studies of serial killers led to a revised view; the killer could have been suspected at the time, but may well have been able to deflect suspicion away from himself. With that in mind, the documents of the day were coupled with our present day understandings and, after discarding the unacceptable maniacs, the following Master Profile took shape:

The killer will not be a person of stature, importance or fame, however:

1. He will be fit, agile, with an icy control; but at the same time will be inclined to be taunting.
2. Not physically distinguished. Neither a giant nor a dwarf.
3. Nothing about him to repel or arouse suspicion.
4. Able to talk easily with prostitutes.
5. He will have an intimate knowledge of the area.
6. Either still living there, or having a retreat there, i.e. a club, institute, friend's or relative's place.

7. Not a surgeon, but with some limited medical knowledge. Maybe a one-time assistant to a GP, or a former medical student.
8. Possibly enjoying some form of cover.
9. Possible past record of deviancy. Perhaps even interviewed by the police of the day.
10. May have talked about the killings.
11. A careful planner, but a high-risk taker.
12. His motives? Perverted sexuality.
13. His career ended by death, disablement or leaving the country.

It was this profile that led directly to the fourth man; an authentic suspect of the time yet neglected. For years muddled researchers had dismissed Roslyn D'Onston as a mere Walter Mitty character. My initial research reinstated him as worthy of study; advanced research revealed him as many times more sinister than my profile, which he had fitted to perfection.

His connections with the murders were multiple; his knowledge of them brands him as *the insider*. Consider just this: on 5 October 1889 the NY 'Police Gazette' listed TWELVE Ripper murders; on 14 February 1891 'The Times' spoke of NINE victims; on 7 March 1891 'Police News' claimed TEN killings. In 1890, by stark contrast, and at a time when the police were still musing about extra Ripper outrages, D'Onston told Cremers this: "There will be no more murders..... you can take it from me that there were no more Ripper murders after that one in Miller's Court on November 9". Both papers and police were woefully wrong, but he was right. And all his other actions and statements are those of a man who knew that the killing-cycle had ended; his physical breakdown now meant that his priority was self-preservation.

Melvin Harris, author of :- Investigating the Unexplained; Jack the Ripper - The Bloody Truth; The Ripper File; The True Face of Jack the Ripper.

Paul Harrison
Noted JTR author and serving police officer

WHO WAS JACK THE RIPPER?

Joseph Barnett, fish porter and paramour of Mary Jane Kelly, was Jack the Ripper; Barnett adored Kelly, he was a rather insecure man, without female company and very much a loner in the East End environment.

Alternately, Kelly was a common whore, a woman who used male companionship to her own devices. Barnett was a mere pawn; Kelly abused his generosity and once he had served all useful purpose she was set to abandon him. Realising this, Barnett was inspired to keep Kelly with him, frightened of once again being alone; the murder of Martha Tabram instilled fear into Kelly and the prostitute community. Barnett realised this was a way to keep the love of his life with him, hence the Ripper murders commenced, each victim carefully pre-selected as a friend of Kelly, thus instilling direct fear.

Eventually, Kelly rejected Barnett; he killed her, refusing to allow anyone else a right to her. Having murdered her and given her a hideous appearance thus ensuring that no one else would want her, he removed her heart, which to his demented mind, could remain with him forever.

There is a great deal of logic in this theory. Other authors have previously claimed that, by the time of the Kelly crime, the Police had narrowed their field of investigation down to a few suspects, the first person brought to, and held after the Kelly murder, was Joe Barnett! The mutilation of the victims was carried out in a direct manner similar to those of a fish porter. Barnett is the only suspect to have been skilled with a knife, to have known at least one victim, to have resided in the area, to have been held by the Police during their investigation.

Paul Harrison. Age 34 years, serving Police Officer with Northamptonshire Police. Has researched the Whitechapel Murders for over 13 years, during which time he has collected and owns many historical documents relating to the crimes, such as the personal correspondence of Inspector Walter Beck, Inspector Frederick Abberline and James McCarthy who found Mary Kelly's remains.
Further to this he owns the only known photograph of his suspect, Joseph Barnett, as well as other personal items allegedly belonging to the man which were received in 1993. Among these was the alleged clay pipe found in Mary Kelly's room and Barnett's personal cut throat razor.
Paul Harrison has written five true crime books; Jack the Ripper The Mystery Solved, Robert Hale 1991. Reprinted 1993. Northamptonshire Murders, Countryside Books 1991. Reprinted 1993.
Yorkshire Murders, Countryside Books 1992.
Devon Murders, Countryside Books 1992.
Hertfordshire/Bedfordshire Murders 1993.
Books for 1994 include;
The Blazing Car Murder; A unique study of the life of A.A. Rouse.
Shropshire Murder Casebook.
He is currently working upon a further book upon the Ripper investigation, for publication in 1995.
OTHER WORKS; Numerous (too many to list) in The Criminologist, Real Life Crimes and How They were Solved, Northamptonshire Evening Telegraph, Chilwell News. Talkthrough, Nene Beat.
He refused to become involved in the 'Ripper Diary' believing it to be a hoax from the outset, classing any further investigation into the matter as "a waste of valuable time." He has appeared on radio in America, Australia, and several local BBC stations around the UK. Further to this he has appeared on Central, Border and Anglia Televisions discussing the Ripper case and appearing in true crime documentaries and research. Presents 'Ripper Talks' to Police Forces around the Globe and to the public on a national basis. His talks have been requested by such agencies as the American FBI, and their German, French and Australian Counterparts.

Shirley Harrison
Narrator of The Diary of Jack the Ripper

WHO WAS JACK THE RIPPER?

In the Spring of 1992 I was commissioned to research and authenticate a sensational diary which had surfaced in Liverpool. It appeared to contain the lurid confessions of Jack the Ripper himself and was probably the most challenging evidence ever to have arisen from the case. The diary has been subjected to unremitting condemnation from "Ripperologists" but has also undergone more intense investigation than any previous Ripper document. Not one shred of firm evidence has yet been produced to prove it a forgery.

After two years, I am personally convinced that the author of the diary was, indeed, James Maybrick, the Liverpool cotton merchant and that Maybrick was Jack the Ripper. His name is already familiar, not as the Ripper but because his wife, Florence, stood trial for poisoning him by arsenic in 1889, the year following the Whitechapel murders. She was sentenced to death, reprieved and served 15 years.

I believe in the diary for many reasons.

Above all, the psychological portrait of a killer that it reveals would have been impossible to simulate and matches what we have discovered about James Maybrick. The diary is the uncontrived product of a tormented mind. And yet there are no mistakes. The ink is right. The paper is right. The history is correct. The medical knowledge revealed is sound.

Two areas are, as yet, unresolved.

In the opinion of handwriting experts, the diary appears not to match the signature on Maybrick's wedding certificate - the only certain example of his handwriting in our possession.

Also, we have been unable to establish the whereabouts of the diary in the last 100 years.

I greeted the appearance of a Victorian watch, just before publication of the hardback version of my book with sceptical alarm. Scratched on the inside back cover were the barely visible words "I am Jack" and the signature "J. Maybrick." I feared a recent forgery. I was wrong. The scratches have been independently examined under an electron microscope at two universities. They are old - probably Victorian. The signature matches the marriage certificate. Together the watch and diary are powerful support for each other - and confirm my belief that James Maybrick was, indeed, Jack the Ripper.

Lifelong contributor to national newspapers and magazines.

Partner in The Word Team - scripting audio - visual presentations, brochures, and graphics for major tourist attractions.

Other books include: "Who is Father Christmas?" (David and Charles) "New Approaches to Cancer" (Century) "The Channel" a history of the dividing link between Britain and France. (Collins) "Cults, the Battle for God". (Christopher Helm).

Extensive U.K. radio and television experience. Coast to Coast exposure on over 100 shows in America, including The Larry King Show, and "60 Minutes"; also media tours of France and Germany.

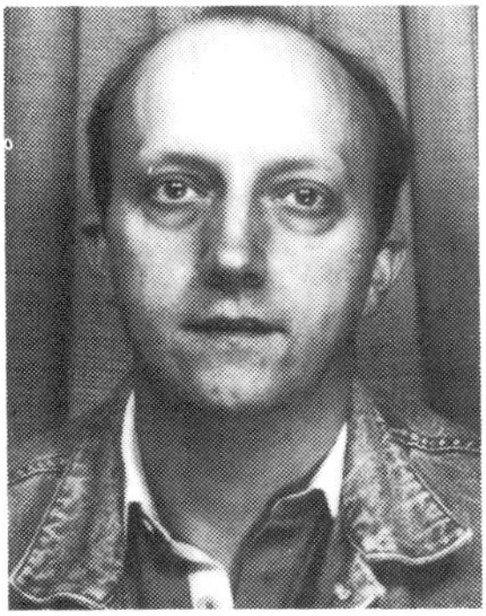

Robert Ives
JTR Enthusiast

A LAYMAN'S VIEW OF JACK THE RIPPER

Why is it that one person can read a book or an article on Jack the Ripper, put it down and forget about it and another will become totally engrossed in the subject and spend years searching for references to it? My interest was sparked by a cartoon strip, Garth, in the Daily Mirror in 1966 and from that moment on I was hooked. I have spent countless hours tracking down books and articles - anything in fact with a reference to Jack. Along the way I have met many weird and wonderful people pursuing the same quest, many of whom have become friends.

There have been some interesting encounters, for instance, in the search for the elusive Whittington-Egan casebook, meeting quite by chance one of his neighbours who told me that the author himself did not have any spare copies and many frustrating experiences such as standing for hours freezing outside train stations waiting to meet fellow collectors and wondering how long it would be before I would get picked up by the police for loitering with intent.

I do not think that there will ever be a definite identification of Jack after all these years but for what it's worth, I am convinced he was Montague John Druitt. I have been of this opinion since reading Daniel Farson's book Jack the Ripper in 1972, wavering only slightly towards Stephen Knight's theory in Jack the Ripper The Final Solution. On reflection, however, I returned once again to Montague John Druitt. There are so many indicators that seem to point to him. We know that the murders were carried out by someone very strong and who must have been quite agile, able to carry out extensive mutilations and still have the energy to slip away quickly and quietly without detection.

Here we have Montague John Druitt, a single man, with no wife to ask awkward questions; he was extremely athletic, a cricketer and former fives player while at Winchester, both sports needing strong arms; he certainly had the opportunity to acquire a basic medical knowledge being the son of a surgeon and having an uncle and cousin who were doctors. His cousin had a surgery in the Minories just a stones throw from Mitre Square. Who knows, Montague may have experienced his first sights and smells of the seedy, stinking slums that existed in Whitechapel when visiting his cousin.

My reasons for supporting Farson's theory were strengthened when thinking about Montague's family. The police certainly seemed to have stopped looking for the murderer after speaking to his brother when Montague's body was found. Sir Melville Macnaghten noted that he had little doubt but that Montague's family suspected him. They must have produced some pretty sound evidence to have convinced the police. The fact that the family approached the police at that stage is very surprising. They had nothing to gain and everything to lose by revealing their suspicions. There was no longer any threat that he might be caught in the act, bringing shame and scandal to the family name; there was no further threat to Whitechapel's "ladies of the night" and they were certainly not looking for any financial reward.

I am of the opinion that they were acting as honest, upright citizens, well aware of the police resources committed to catching the murderer and they "did the right thing" by informing the authorities, in the apparently well founded belief, that their position would be respected and the family name protected and the file could be closed.

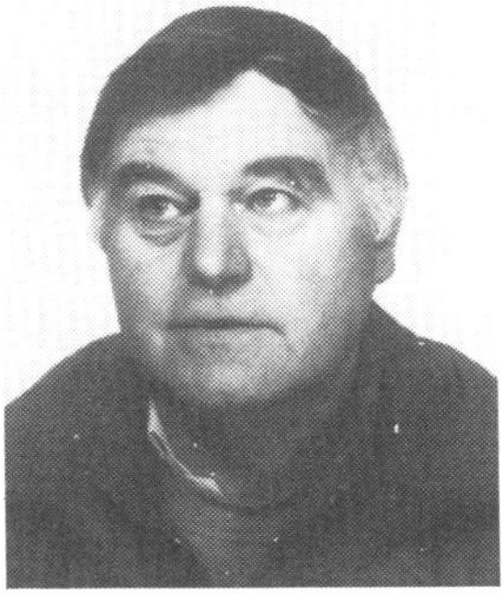

Allan Jones
JTR Enthusiast

THE IDENTITY OF JACK THE RIPPER???

May I start by saying that I have no books to sell, nor do I anticipate writing any; I have no particular wish to be interviewed on radio or television and, to be honest, I really have no idea who Jack the Ripper was or if anybody else, apart from Jack and possibly some of his victims, ever really knew either. I think I can reasonably lay claim to having read most of the material worth reading (and much that is not) which is in any way connected with this century-old mystery.

Ripper students, I have noticed, vary considerably in their willingness to accept or reject the comments of those who were much closer to the events than we are. For those who worked on the case, I have varying degrees of respect. Major Henry Smith of the City Police, who was probably *not* amongst the greatest policemen of his day, did admit in his memoirs of 1910, that the Ripper "Completely beat me and every police officer in London". Contrary to Smith, the eminent Robert Anderson, who also wrote his memoirs in 1910, asserted that the Ripper's identity was "a definitely ascertained fact". Added support for Anderson came to light in recent years with the discovery of written comments by Chief Inspector Donald Swanson. In spite of these excellent sources, I feel that we are dealing with yet another suspect who would not detain a modern judge and jury for very long.

An important issue to me is the number of victims claimed for the Ripper. I have never been absolutely certain who, in Anderson's opinion, were victims of Jack, and who were not. In 1894 Melville Macnaghten, who was not a police officer in 1888, effectively wrote the "rule-book" which today's participants in the game of "Hunt the Ripper" play by. Macnaghten limited the number of murders, committed by Jack, to five : Nicholls, Chapman, Stride, Eddowes, and Kelly. This is probably the one feature of Macnaghten's beliefs most widely accepted today, though apparently this was not a view shared by all who were involved at the time.

The recent discovery of a journal, claimed to have been written by the Ripper, may or may not be genuine. If it is not, then it still has to be noted that the writer is careful not to invite disbelief by contradicting Macnaghten's opinions regarding the five East End murders. Very few modern writers, it seems, are prepared to argue with Macnaghten on the subject of the number of Ripper victims, but I do wonder why it is so widely accepted that Jack didn't mutilate Liz Stride because he was interrupted in his work. Surely this is more of a theory than a fact? Why could the Ripper not have killed Martha Tabram or Alice McKenzie? With respect, I don't quite see how Macnaghten could have been so sure.

In February 1891, the murder of Frances Coles brought both Anderson and Macnaghten to the scene of the crime. Does this suggest that the identity of the 1888 murderer might not have been as clear in their minds as it apparently became later on?

In closing I would like to express my thanks to so many other Ripper students, over the years. Their boundless enthusiasm, if not always their sense of direction, has been a constant source of inspiration.

Colin Kendell
JTR Enthusiast

WHO WAS JACK THE RIPPER?

Jack the Ripper seemed to follow the classic pattern of serial murderers. He began tentatively - his first victim was mutilated to a far lesser degree than the later ones - he quickly gained confidence and began to take "trophies" in the shape of organs removed from his victims, and "depersonalised" the last two by disfiguring their faces. Most serial killers go on killing until they are caught, however, Jack the Ripper stopped.

The evidence, particularly the post mortem mutilation of his victims, suggested the introverted, woman-hating type of murderer, but that may have been the impression that was meant to be created. There was far more planning involved in the murders than the police at the time realised - or admitted - and the most notable example of this was the fourth. The victim, Catherine Eddowes, was found extensively mutilated in Aldgate's Mitre Square, where police patrols in and around the square restricted the time available to the murderer to five minutes. The post mortem report said that whole of that time would have been taken up by the careful nicking of the victim's eyelids with the point of a knife.

Eddowes must therefore have been brought to the square already dead and mutilated. Her throat had obviously been cut there - practically the only wound she received that could have been inflicted in the dark. It would have been possible to find the throat by touch and then cut it. The post mortem report suggests that this was done clumsily and at the second attempt, probably reflecting the difficulty created by the darkness. This would have been done to give the impression that she had been murdered where she was found. Modern experts would call this creating false evidence "staging".

The police had all the evidence available but persisted with the line that Eddowes had been murdered in Mitre Square. Four days after the final murder Abberline, the detective in charge, abandoned the investigation, apparently knowing that the Ripper had killed for the last time. This is one of the reasons for the feeling which has always persisted that more was known about the murders than was admitted.

The late Stephen Knight's theory that the victims knew of the Duke of Clarence's secret marriage and were murdered, in Masonic style, by Dr. Gull in a coach is badly flawed in background detail and the source is suspect. It is, however, the only explanation which has answered all the questions and only came to light through a Scotland Yard tip-off. Gull was known to be sadistic, ruthless and possessed of a bizarre sense of humour. It has been denied that he was a Freemason himself but it might have amused him to embarrass high ranking members of the Brotherhood, such as Warren, the Commissioner of the Metropolitan Police, by re-enacting Masonic executions on the streets of London, As a man who had succeeded entirely by his own abilities, he would have resented them attaining positions through nepotism.

There are two documented instances of him removing organs from dead patients against their families' wishes, and in one instance he did so in the most brutal manner - perhaps feeling that their ignorance in opposing him should be punished. If he did devise and commit the Ripper murders he may have felt echoes of those past battles against ignorance when he removed organs from the women in Whitechapel.

Published Works

"Did Mary Kelly Die?"
The Criminologist 1988

"Jack the Ripper - 1988 And All That"
The Criminologist 1989

"The Intentions of Thomas Eldon Stowell"
The Criminologist 1990

"Comedy of Omissions"
The Criminologist 1990

Ray Luff
JTR Enthusiast

JACK THE RIPPER

After thirty-five years of being interested in the Whitechapel murders, I can offer no definitive answer as an explanation of the Ripper killings. The enduring fascination of Jack the Ripper lies in the fact that the mystery does seem to be insoluble and likely to remain so. I was once convinced that Montague John Druitt was the most likely suspect, but with the latest research indicating the thinking of Sir Robert Anderson and Donald Swanson - the men in the best position to know - I would tend to support conclusions based on this line of enquiry - though I feel the case against Kosminski is far from proven. I feel the most promising new information is the suspect named by Inspector John Littlechild, Head of the Secret Department at Scotland Yard. If further research can place his American suspect at the scenes of other Ripper-like killings elsewhere, this must rank as one of the strongest pointers to the killer's identity ever proposed. If it is true that serial killers of the Ripper's type do go on killing unless they die or are incarcerated, then the Littlechild suspect would very likely have continued killing after leaving the country following Kelly's murder in 1888. However, if research leads us up a blind (Whitechapel) alley, then I would have to cast my vote for a local Whitechapel inhabitant - not necessarily an immigrant - who was, in the words of Arthur Douglas "a mere nobody after all"

I do believe Elizabeth Stride *was* a victim of Jack the Ripper, despite the current line of thought that suggests otherwise. The description of the man who assaulted Stride in Berner Street as given by Schwartz, is so close to the description of the man seen with Eddowes at Mitre Square by Lawende, that I believe both witnesses are describing the actual murderer. However, despite the LWT "Crime Monthly" "portrait" of Jack the Ripper as an ordinary-looking man in a short jacket and peaked cap, the popular image of "Jack" will most likely remain that of the top-hatted, cloaked villain disappearing into the (non-existent) swirling fog. The legend of Jack the Ripper will undoubtedly win out over the historical reality - despite the ongoing work of first-class writers and researchers.

I first became interested in Jack the Ripper in 1959. In that year Donald McCormick's book was published, a British black and white film called "Jack the Ripper" was on general release at cinemas, and Daniel Farson's TV series featured Jack's crimes and included the suspect's initials on screen: M.J.D.

In 1965 I explored the district regularly and visited the murder sites which, apart from Berner Street and Dorset Street, remained pretty much as they appeared in 1888. One felt a strong presence of Jack the Ripper in particular in walking through the passage that led from the front door of 29 Hanbury Street to the rear yard which had hardly changed in the 77 years since Annie Chapman breathed her last there. On a visit to St. Patrick's Roman Catholic Cemetery, a clerk responded to my request to see the burial entry for Mary Kelly by producing a ledger from a safe and turning up the entry which showed Kelly's name entered under the french variant of Marie Jeanette.

I have no writing on the subject published beyond letters in various magazines and latterly in "Ripperana". In the 1960s I took photographs and colour slides at the remaining Ripper sites and more recently I made videos of the streets in Whitechapel and Spitalfields and also videos of some of the leading writers on Jack the Ripper.

Peter McLeave
JTR Enthusiast

WHO WAS JACK THE RIPPER?

Of all murder mysteries, the Whitechapel killings of 1888 continue to hold a contemporary audience rapt over a century later. This says as much about us as about the perpetrator, for the circumstances of that series form a psychologically charged backdrop before which to play out our own fantasies and fears. Any announcement of the definitive solution is greeted with hoots of derision from other committed quarters. But Jack will not be nailed. 'Yours truly', our 'independent genius' as Bernard Shaw described him, will remain anonymous for posterity.

If motivation is the most important factor in any crime, then the Whitechapel murders are at once problematical. The old chestnuts of gain, sexual jealousy and revenge won't do in themselves and need expansion. Obviously there was no gain from prostitutes. Sexual jealousy is cited by some - the Barnett theory, for instance - overlapping revenge which, in some form, has always seemed the most attractive notion. If Jack's motivation is a lottery, then better to look at the circumstances of the murders, and particularly the carnage in Miller's Court, a literal and metaphorical catharsis.

The shock and revulsion that most people experience on first seeing *that* photograph of the Kelly murder never lessens. It is frankly difficult to believe that one human being meted out such treatment to another. Yet the intensity and savagery, the thoroughness and resolve of the attack are a clue to the mystery. This is no random selection, no casual encounter ending in mayhem. This is the destruction, or rather deconstruction. of another individual. We know of dismemberment - Mahon, Thorne and Ruxton being prime examples - and sadism as found in the Heath case. But surely none of these sought to destroy all trace of the victim as at Miller's Court. A point was being made, an example held up for others to remark, that this was what could happen.

So why were five prostitutes murdered that fateful autumn? I believe Kelly needed to be silenced for her own sake and to discourage others of a like persuasion. (We know the penultimate victim, Eddowes, was also known as Mary Kelly). Kelly had some knowledge that might damage or undermine those with most to lose. Either that, or she had compromised an important client and had talked, or threatened to talk. This is familiar as part of Knight's defamed theory without the royal dimension. The murderer had some skill with the knife, certainly so to remove Eddowes's kidney.

The nature of the mutilations are crucial. The internal organs, severed and deposited outside the body, take on a ritual significance and, when considered in the light of the Goulston Street graffito and Warren's premature erasure, indicate a strong Freemasonic element. To render the word 'Juwes' in any other form seems disingenuous, and I don't think that a pogrom was uppermost in Warren's mind, rather a knowledge after the fact. Nicholls, Chapman and Stride may have been the prelude to the real work at hand, or they may also have 'known too much', including Kelly's intimacies. A string of suspects give the appearance of activity. Pizer and Pedachenko, Kosminski and Druitt, all conveniently placed and all fall guys. Conspiracy theories are unfashionable but the motivation at Miller's Court was, above everything else, punishment.

Donald McCormick
Noted author on JTR

THE IDENTITY OF JACK THE RIPPER

Dr. Thomas Dutton compiled, over a period of 60 years, three volumes of hand-written "Chronicles of Crime" based on his experiences as a doctor. Dr.Dutton and Chief-Inspector Abberline of Scotland Yard were friends. Dutton suggested that if Abberline was looking for a foreigner, he should look for one who might pass as an Englishman - "I would keep a special watch on Poles and Russians".

One day Abberline called at a hairdresser's shop in Whitechapel, the assistant was called Klosowski and had been a feldscher in the Russian Army. A feldscher is an assistant to a doctor in Poland and Russia.

In Dutton's Diaries he says "I have learned, from a French doctor, of a Russian junior surgeon, or feldscher, who was known to him in Paris about 1885-8. He was suspected of having killed and mutilated a 'grisette' in Montmartre, but he left Paris before he could be arrested". This surgeon whose name was Konovalov, was said to have a violent hatred of prostitutes. The description of Konovalov exactly fits that of Pedachenko and the final police assessment of what the Ripper looked like.

The killer may have had male and female disguises. Though the various men seen with the Ripper victims shortly before each crime were physically alike, their attire was somewhat different. The more one considers the possibility of the murderer disguising himself as a woman, the more probable it seems; while many witnesses saw a man in the vicinity just before each murder, no one saw a man immediately afterwards. The only possible exception is in the case of Elizabeth Stride, but even then it is not certain whether Mrs. Mortimer saw the man just before or just after the murder.

Then there was the killer's halt at the close near Dorset Street to wash his hands in the sink after the Eddowes murder; it is feasible that he stopped more for the purpose of changing his clothes. Nobody mentioned seeing a woman in the vicinity of these crimes, but the explanation may be that nobody was looking for a female, even had they noticed one, they would not have referred to her. Would the two women who claimed to have seen Mary Kelly after she was murdered have invented their stories? Mrs. Maxwell agreed that Kelly was all muffled up.

How four of the Ripper victims mentioned by Dr. Dutton should come to be visiting a clinic in Walworth is not explained. The doctor stated that he made the discovery from Dr. J. F. Williams, who lived in Camberwell, and attended St Saviour's Infirmary; he said that a Russian surgeon assisted him occasionally. This man's name was Pedachenko. Pedachenko did not attend the clinic at St. Saviour's Infirmary after Mary Kelly's murder. Williams said that Pedachenko was ambidextrous - so was the Ripper.

If as seems likely, the Russian surgeon had made the acquaintance of some of these women at the clinic, this might be one reason why they would be unafraid to venture down dark alleys with him.

At one time the author had in his possession a letter from a female in Canada who claimed to have been married to Jack the Ripper!

'The Identity of Jack the Ripper' by Donald McCormick. New and Revised Edn. 1970. Grey House Books has, with the author's permission, used his own words to explain his theories on the identity of Jack the Ripper.

Mark Madden
JTR Enthusiast

MY EXPLANATION OF THE RIPPER KILLINGS

The few facts known about Jack the Ripper are that he was local as he knew all the possible short cuts to roam around Whitechapel without detection. Also because of being a native, there must have been something disarming about him for women to approach him, considering that by the time of Annie Chapman's murder, the press were saying that at least three prostitutes had been killed by the same man. He had skill with a knife and he was possibly a slaughterman, fishmonger or porter.

Mary Jane Kelly's lover Joseph Barnett and brother Daniel Barnett as possible accomplice, are the only known plausible candidates. Joseph Barnett was a fish porter and riverside labourer. Brother Daniel was a fishmonger and also porter. Joseph at the time of Kelly's inquest said he was living at his sister's flat at 21 Portpool Lane in Holborn. Brother Daniel's work record shows that he lived at this address from 1884 to 1892. There is no record in the 1881 and 1891 census returns for sister Catherine living at this address.

The night before Mary Kelly was murdered, a Maurice Lewis said he saw Julia and Dan, a porter from Billingsgate Market, drinking with her. Also that night, Joseph visited Kelly at Millers Court on the pretext to say that he had no money to give her. A week earlier he left because of her allowing prostitutes to stay overnight at Millers Court, which was his home. Another reason given as to why he left her was because he didn't like Kelly soliciting. This was confirmed by witness Julia Venturey at the inquest. Lizzie Albrook said that Kelly was sick of the way her life was going, which for the past 18 months had been in the company of Joe Barnett, and that she wanted to go home to her people in Ireland. It is worth noting that she didn't say Wales which is allegedly where she grew up.

After the row with Kelly, when the famous window was conveniently broken, Joe Barnett left her to live five minutes away in New Street, Bishopsgate. Forensic evidence suggests that Mary Kelly had retired for the night and was killed in her sleep. Whoever was the last person to be with her in Millers Court, Dorset Street, must have known that she would be alone that night, as the other women had found other accommodation a day or so before. Joe Barnett would have known this as he had been visiting every day since leaving her.

Joe Barnett couldn't let her go, but he couldn't tolerate her soliciting - and letting prostitutes stay overnight in their room, was more than he could cope with. Being out of work, which was the reason why Kelly returned to the streets, for at least three months, was more than Barnett could tolerate, and so went out on a rampage to let out his anger. He killed and mutilated Mary Ann Nichols, Annie Chapman, possibly Elizabeth Stride, Catherine Eddowes. All these women stood for everything he hated in Mary Kelly. Sometime in August something in his mind snapped and Joe Barnett started to vent his anger.

The reason why he killed Mary Kelly I think was simply that, if he couldn't have her then nobody would. His love was an obessional love, and he had the early start of a disturbed childhood, which can often be the base of psychopathic behaviour.

On the night of Catherine Eddowes' murder, the murderer was heading north in Goulston Street. Opposite lay Bell Lane which ran into Crispin Street - this ran parallel to Dorset Street. Major Henry Smith claimed that he found a blood stained sink in Dorset Street, where only a local person would have been able to know about its location, on the same night. Joe Barnett was living in Dorset Street at this time.

A book entitled "The Mystery of Jack the Ripper", Published in 1929, when people alive could still remember the Autumn of 1888, concluded that the reason for the murders was because of Mary Kelly. I feel sure that Mary Kelly was the reason for the Jack the Ripper murders. Why else did the murders stop? When Joe Barnett moved from Whitechapel to live in Holborn, the murders also ended.

Contributor and mention in the Introduction "The Jack the Ripper - A to Z" Revised Edn. - 1994.

Christopher Missen
Researcher on Serial Sex Killers

WHO WAS JACK THE RIPPER?

The identity of Jack the Ripper can never be incontrovertibly established. But from the data obtained from a survey of more than 1500 US and UK serial sex killers, certain traits of the real Jack the Ripper may be logically inferred.
(ssk = serial sex killer).

Conclusions Up to Date
Privileged classes unlikely to be implicated.
Jill the Ripper can be repudiated.
Middle-class ssks are all but non-existent.
Ssks feel that they have nothing to lose. That rules out dissolute Royals or their medical appointees, or high court judges.

A Number of Jack the Ripper's Likely Characteristics can be Catalogued :
1. Jack would have resided in the immediate vicinity.
2. Jack would have been an habitual drinker, prone to aggressive outbursts after drinking.
3. Married but estranged from spouse. Subject to irrational unprovoked explosions of jealousy.
4. Naturally clever rather than intelligent.
5. Accentuates Philistinism to ingratiate himself with low life characters.
6. Unable to keep any job for long, due to clashes with superiors.
7. Abnormal height. More likely to be tall as evidenced by Liz Stride's shoulder bruises.
8. Well known locally, especially to police. Burglary, drink, violent or sexual offences etc.
9. May have been institutionalised early in life.

10. Lacked childhood bliss.
11. Childhood overshadowed by dominant mother.
12. Probably Catholic upbringing, some victims were Catholic. Parents may have been displaced persons. Rippers, unlike many other types of carnal predators, are most often intra-ethnic.
13. If Jack was English he may well have been a comparative newcomer to the East End.
14. Most likely to be 28 - 40 years of age.
15. He would NOT have written any of the missives attributed to him. ALL (so called) RIPPER LETTERS ARE HOAXES. He was a dweller in the shadows.
16. Jack would not have been described as demented by associates. Maybe Jack only exhibited manic behavioural symptoms when intoxicated. On such occasions he would shun company and evidently disappear.
17. Excessively class and status conscious. Never apologises or admits errors.
18. Likely to have been a regular patron of a class of whore similar to those he butchered.
19. Excessively repressed and tried to ignore or deny his secret vices. Traits may be more or less repressed homosexuality or bisexuality. Maybe suspected of paedophile propensities (even incest).
20. Outwardly sexually normal. Capable of performing conventional sex acts.
21. Will have tried to control chronic and ever intensifying destructive lusts. May be lengthy intervals between outrages.
22. Known fascination with collection of weaponry in general. May have had jobs requiring the use of a knife.
23. Frequent and sudden change of address whilst remaining in same vicinity.
24. Initial violent outbursts, March, April, or August 1888 likely to have been preceded by personal crisis.
25. ALMOST CERTAIN TO HAVE BEEN INTERVIEWED AT LEAST ONCE BY RIPPER INVESTIGATORS, perhaps as a known prowler, or partner of whores.
26. OVERTLY RACIST - likely to have been actively ANTI-SEMITIC.
27. History of domestic disturbances.
28. Not suicidal. Ssks only kill themselves when they know the 'jig is up'.
29. Likely to have been in custody. Likely to have served in the military within previous 5 years.
30. NOTABLY CRUEL TO ANIMALS, especially as a juvenile.

Author and historic-document consultant Joe Nickell assists forensic document examiner Maureen Casey Owens in conducting an analysis of the 'Jack the Ripper Diary.'

Dr. Joe Nickell
American author and historic-document consultant

WHO WAS JACK THE RIPPER?

Sometime in 1991, a Liverpool scrap-metal dealer named Mike Barrett allegedly came into possession of a remarkable item, the diary of one of the world's most maniacal serial killers. If genuine, the volume solved the century-old mystery of London's Whitechapel murders, proving that the fiend who reportedly styled himself "Jack the Ripper" had been a 50-year-old cotton merchant from Liverpool, James Maybrick (who died of poison in 1889).

Barrett sought to capitalize on his find, and soon Robert Smith of Smith Gryphon Publishers was announcing a forthcoming book edited by Shirley Harrison. It was to be co-published in the United States by Warner Books and titled *The Diary of Jack the Ripper : The Discovery, the Investigation and the Authentication.* Almost immediately, however, sceptics questioned the reported "authentication," and at the eleventh hour, with the text already set in type, Warner executives sought to obtain their own expert opinion. They naturally turned to Kenneth Rendell, the manuscript authority who investigated the notorious "Hitler Diaries" for *Newsweek* magazine. Rendell in turn contacted me and, while arrangements were made for the diary to be insured for $1 million and brought to the United States, I proceeded to secure a forensic laboratory and to assemble a team of ink chemists and other experts. On August 21, 1993, we met at the Chicago laboratory of noted handwriting expert Maureen Casey Owens.

We determined the diary was an obvious forgery, based primarily on conclusive handwriting evidence but also indicated by a number of suspicious features. These include a non-existent provenance: Barrett claimed the diary was given him by a drinking buddy, since deceased, whose family, however, denied any knowledge of it. In addition, the leather-bound volume was not manufactured as a diary but instead as a scrapbook. The first two dozen pages have been cut out and the remaining blank pages used for the "diary" — an unlikely thing for Maybrick to do; with his wealth he would surely have bought a proper Victorian diary. Moreover, brown rectangular stains on the flyleaf and other clues indicate that the scrapbook had held post-Victorian roll-film photographs — evidence incompatible with Maybrick's authorship. The text of the diary is also suspect, its author frequently going out of his way to include some detail — such as the empty tin match box that belonged to victim Catherine Eddowes — that seems intended to impress Ripper researchers. Yet all such details are found in published books on the Whitechapel murders. The most significant evidence is provided by the handwriting. Not only is it excessively variable for a natural hand, but it fails to match either that of a "Jack the Ripper" letter of 1888 (which the diary deliberately associates itself with) or the actual handwriting of James Maybrick as found on his marriage certificate and his holographic will. (Robert Smith's claim that it is the *will* that is a forgery is absurd.) The writing skill evidenced by the diary is far inferior to that of James Maybrick or to the author of the "Jack the Ripper" letter.

About the time Warner cancelled publication, we learned that prior to our examination *The Sunday Times* of London had already assembled its own panel of experts who likewise determined the diary was a fake. Smith Gryphon attempted to hold the newspaper to a confidentiality agreement (signed in connection with an option on serial rights), but the latter issued a writ in the High Court — citing fraud and misrepresentation — and prevailed.

On September 19, 1993, *The Sunday Times* published a two-page expose, "Fake!" One bombshell was that Smith had withheld an early report prepared for him by an experienced forensic document expert, David Baxendale, who determined the diary was a modern fake. For example, Baxendale did an ink-solubility test which indicated — more accurately, in my opinion, than a controversial test our team commissioned — that the writing had probably been done within the past three years. Notwithstanding Robert Smith's manner of dealing with it, the evidence is clear and compelling. Neither James Maybrick nor any other candidate for Ripperhood could have written a diary a century after the events this amateurish fake purports to describe.

Joe Nickell, Ph.D., is a historic-document consultant and author of several books, including an acclaimed reference work on writing and writing materials (*Pen, Ink and Evidence,* 1990)

Robin Odell
Noted True Crime author including JTR

NO STRANGER TO THE KNIFE

In all the millions of words written about Jack the Ripper, what is there that can be relied upon? Very little, do I hear you say? But, surely, among all the fact, fiction, and fantasy, there must lie some nuggets of truth. Yet, it hardly seems possible, after all this time, that anything worthwhile has been overlooked.

The answer might be found not in something that has been missed but in what may have been too easily dismissed. Considering the murders in a purely contemporary context, whose on-the-spot observations might be expected to carry weight? Probably the police officers and doctors who examined the crime scenes. And, of the two, one might opt for the doctors as professionals with scientific knowledge who were trained to observe and interpret.

So what did the doctors, those first-hand observers at the Ripper scenes-of-crimes, have to say?

Doctor Rees Ralph Llewellyn, the Whitechapel general practitioner who examined the wounds inflicted on Mary Ann Nichols, concluded that they were "deftly and skilfully performed".

In the case of Annie Chapman, the doctor at the scene was George Bagster Phillips, a police surgeon of twenty years' experience. He carried out the post mortem examination on her body and concluded that the murderer had "... such knowledge of anatomical or pathological examinations as to be enabled to secure the pelvic organs with one sweep of the knife".

The murderer is supposed to have been disturbed while despatching his third victim, Elizabeth Stride, hence there were no mutilations apart from the cut throat.

Next came Catherine Eddowes on the same night as Stride, whose extensive wounds, including the removal of a kidney, provided ample scope for medical observation. Dr Frederick Gordon Brown, The City of London police surgeon, was rather definite in his opinion "the perpetrator of the crime possessed some anatomical knowledge". Dr George William Sequiera believed that the murderer showed no more knowledge than would be expected of a professional butcher and added "He was no stranger to the knife". Dr William Sedgwick Saunders, who assisted at the post mortem on Eddowes, was inclined to agree with Dr Brown, although not wholly.

The shredded remains of Mary Kelly offered little prospect of observing evidence of technique but Dr Thomas Bond stated that he saw no indications of "scientific or anatomical knowledge".

What all this seems to demonstrate is that of the six medical opinions expressed at the time, four were in favour of some notion of skill, one was tentative and one was totally against. This looks rather like a consensus that cannot easily be dismissed as irrelevant.

Surely, the knowledgeable views of experienced medical men who saw the victims' injuries at first hand must be in a different class to latter day pundits occupying distant armchairs and looking at faded photographs?

I am not suggesting that Jack the Ripper was a doctor or a surgeon. I am saying that his skill with a knife, particularly in the matter of throat cutting, was commensurate with the technique of a butcher or a slaughterer. I know that the police investigated slaughter houses in Whitechapel at the time of the murders. But what could they possibly have expected to find except men with knives in their hands and blood on their clothes?

ODELL, Robin : JACK THE RIPPER IN FACT AND FICTION, Harrap, London 1965

ODELL, Robin : JACK THE RIPPER, Paper presented to Our Society, London, May 1976

WILSON, Colin and ODELL, Robin : JACK THE RIPPER: SUMMING UP AND VERDICT, Bantam, London, 1987

Jon Ogan
JTR Enthusiast

AN APPRAISAL OF THE WHITECHAPEL MURDERS

Sir Robert Anderson, the Assistant Commissioner of the Metropolitan Police described the opinion: "That a crime such as this kind should have been committed without any clue being supplied by the criminal is unusual, but that FIVE successive murders should have been committed without our having the slightest clue of any kind is extraordinary, if not unique in the annals of crime". (Home Office document: 23-10-1888). Which for their contemporary setting would have been a perplexing series of murders.

Indeed, there was a lack of ability in being able to identify 'bona fide' victims of the Whitechapel Murderer. Press speculation attempted to link a set of ten murders and attribute them to the hand of 'Jack the Ripper.' A name taken from a number of letters allegedly written by the offender.

In the present day, modern psychological techniques can be used to understand something of the personality of the perpetrator, and aid in forming a 'pen picture' of the offender's occupational status and geographical location in relation to the crime scene. All of which would have been alien to Anderson and his contemporaries. Prof. David Canter's book **Criminal Shadows** (Harper Collins, 1994) provides a very readable account of the application of these techniques used to prioritise police suspects, experience gained at first hand in assisting police enquiries into a number of offences. The book does give a brief discussion of the Whitechapel Murders. However, Prof. Canter provided more details on the likely offender type for use in the articles appearing in Nos. 8 & 9 of **"Ripperana".**

Canter summarised the characteristics of the suspect as : The first crime attributed to the Whitechapel murderer would not have been the first crime he committed. Some psychological disturbance would have been noted by the suspect's associates; the suspect would have lived amidst/adjacent to the crime scenes. He would also be regarded as a man difficult to relate to, but would have been capable of holding down a job needing some skill in communicating albeit at a basic level. The above aspects represent a broad, but useful outline of the likely suspect.

The crimes themselves can be analysed to provide a core series of homicides numbering 4-6 likely victims these are: Tabram(?), Nichols, Chapman, Stride(?), Eddowes & Kelly.

Further crimes may also be considered as they reflect an escalating or progressive nature of mutilations. For instance, Tabram/Turner was the least planned crime; the subsequent murder of Nichols showed that the offender had ensured less blood spillage, but the nature of the attack and mutilation is indicative of a strong relationship between the crimes. It should also be noted that Anderson's communiqué pre-dated the Kelly murder, and consequently has implications for the inclusion of Tabram/Turner. Consequently, the attacks on Wilson and others can also be considered for inclusion, and provide useful physical evidence from a surviving victim.

Clearly, rather than concerning ourselves with the suspect's identity at the present confused state, we should first ensure that the relevant homicides are identified and examined for all pertinent information that can be used to point to the most realistic offender type. Therefore, the use of 'offender profiling' is not advocated here to replace the excellent historical research that has been achieved so far, but to augment it by providing an investigative framework to follow.

Published articles

PHS Journal Vol. 5 (1990) Martha Tabram- the forgotten Ripper Victim?
Ripperana July 1993: John William Sanders MD
Ripperana Dec 1993: A light in the shadows (pt 1)
Ripperana April 1994: A light in the shadows (pt 2)

To be published (?): Tabram Tabulated.

Claudia Oliver
JTR author

WHAT HAPPENED TO MARY JANE KELLY?

My interest in Jack the Ripper began when I was fourteen. I never once believed Mary Kelly was murdered and have been unable to ignore facts which have come to light. If you read non-biased accounts they are all too obvious.

Many theorists turn a blind eye to evidence which does not conform to their ideas. My desire for the truth resulted in a theory which emphasises Mary's role. Joseph Barnett said she spoke of being afraid of someone, of being cut down by the Ripper.

Mary told him that family resided in London. Her account of her life was full of (deliberate?) fabrications. As McCarthy her landlord pointed out, she received letters from Ireland. This was borne out by Lizzie Albrook, a friend of Mary's who said:

'.....she was sick of the life she was leading and wished to go back to Ireland where her people lived'.

Julia Venturney said she was fond of a man named Joe. There were also suggestions of a man who ill-used Mary and hit her. But surely the most important evidence was provided by Caroline Maxwell who spoke to Mary eight hours after her 'death'. There was also a reported change in Mary's attire that night and she was seen in Dorset Street's Brittannia at 10.00 a.m., the murder being discovered at 10.45 a.m.

Medical testimony has helped in defining this evidence. The time of death was estimated at between 1 and 2 a.m. A cry of 'Oh Murder' was heard at 4.00 a.m. It is unlikely a person being attacked would cry out this way. It would however, be more indicative on discovery of a body.

It was known that Mary was three months pregnant, yet the post-mortem revealed the organs for such a thing to have occurred to be present and correct. Yet another fact which lends doubt as to the identity of the victim. Few people could overlook such evidence, and yet they do.

Barnett, who identified the body, felt certain it was she. Take a look at the face of the corpse. Could you ascertain without a shadow of a doubt, its true identity? I would conclude that Mary discovered the body and fled the district with whoever 'Jack' was.

In 1993 I chose a name for the body buried in Leytonstone Cemetery. She was originally identified in the diaries of Inspector Abberline as Winnifred May Collis, who vanished in 1888. It was alleged she had been an acquaintance of Mary's. So what happened to Mary Kelly? I believe her to have returned to Ireland. If, by Lizzie's evidence, she were that desperate, if someone were to provide the money, would she have fled? And who provided the financial aid that would take her across the sea? One point that sticks in my mind is that 'Jack' disappeared after the last murder, after Mary Kelly had seemingly vanished into thin air. I would consider the Ripper to be a boyfriend of Mary's, left in the lurch when she favoured another. The resulting blackmail and emotional threats turned into murder. Reports named a man known only as 'Morganstone' to be a one time lover of Mary's. As she was fond of keeping up with past affections was he overlooked by the authorities and was he the same man who ill used her. I'd expect to find the answer in Ireland.

A book, **'The Kelly Connection'** is in its final draft, and I am looking to produce the film version, **'A Truth Unknown'.**

Bruce Paley
JTR author

THEORY ON THE JACK THE RIPPER MURDERS

A lifelong East Ender, Joseph Barnett worked as a fish porter at Billingsgate Market, there becoming proficient with a knife and gaining a rough knowledge of anatomy through cleaning and gutting fish. In 1887 he moved in with the alcoholic prostitute Mary Jane Kelly after only their second meeting. The arrangement suited them both: to Barnett, still single at 29 and afflicted with a speech impediment, the young, attractive Kelly represented quite a catch and he took great pride in keeping her off the streets, while to a woman in Kelly's position, the value of a solid wage earner like Barnett was considerable. Kelly may have also been impressed by Barnett's education and respectable appearance which set him above others of his class.

Barnett claimed that he and Kelly lived together comfortably, but in actuality the couple had frequent heated rows sparked by Kelly's drinking. Barnett also disapproved of her prostitute friends and Kelly's continued liaisons with her former beau. Eventually Kelly came to despise Barnett, only staying with him because he was a good provider and treated her well indulging her with money and gifts - until he inexplicably lost his job, which forced Kelly back into prostitution. It was an intolerable situation for Barnett: he couldn't bear for Kelly to be on the streets, yet it was his own failure and inadequacy as a provider that had forced Kelly back into prostitution. Barnett also knew that without his earnings he was expendable but short of finding another well paying job - an impossibility given the local high unemployment - Barnett could see no way out of his predicament, until Kelly's fearful reaction to the brutal murder of a local prostitute may have provided him with a desperate solution. Afraid of losing Kelly, while tormented by overwhelming sexual jealousy, frustration, low self-esteem and a hatred of prostitutes, Barnett thus set out to *frighten* Kelly off the streets, (and give her need of him again), by butchering her fellow prostitutes. So great was Kelly's fear of the killer, that she would have Barnett read her the latest developments of the case from the newspapers. Knowing then that Kelly was assured of hearing of them, Barnett thus sent the gruesome Jack the Ripper letters to the *Central News Agency*, (in which he singled out prostitutes as his intended targets), rather than to the police.

As a familiar local figure Barnett could approach his potential victims without alarming them and may have even known them, as three of the murdered women had been living in Dorset Street at the time of their deaths, where Barnett and Kelly lived. On the night of the double murder, the Ripper allegedly left a trail leading to that same small street, while two reliable eyewitness sightings that night produced an *exact description of Joseph Barnett.* At some point, Barnett had also lived near *all* of the murder sites, - a knowledge that served him well, as the Ripper was nearly set upon twice. After the double murder, Kelly finally refrained from prostitution, and there followed the longest gap between murders since they had begun, until a violent quarrel saw Barnett move out, evidently taking the key to their room with him. He expected to move back in shortly, though Kelly, morose and despondent, possibly pregnant, could no longer bear Barnett, and wouldn't have him back. Ten days after he left Barnett visited a drunken Kelly in the middle of the night and after she apparently rejected him, savagely murdered her, locking the door behind him when he left. Jack the Ripper was never heard from again, and at Kelly's inquest, Barnett's anxiety and nervousness were noted, though his contradictory statements as to why he and Kelly had parted went unnoticed.

In common with the mould of today's serial killers, Barnett was a white male in his 20s or 30s, from a dysfunctional family marked by the loss of his father (when Barnett was six), and a distant mother. As is often the case, Barnett suffered from a physical disability, and toiled in a menial job beneath his intelligence, (though one which facilitated his morbid fantasies), the loss of which helped to trigger the murders.

My theory - the first to implicate Joseph Barnett - was initially published in the April, 1982 edition of True Crime, and has since been discussed in several subsequent Jack the Ripper books. I have recently finished a book on Barnett and the Ripper murders, (which identifies his living descendants), and am currently seeking a publisher.

Donald Rumbelow
Noted True Crime author including JTR

WHO WAS JACK THE RIPPER?

It was not a particular theory that impelled me to write 'The Complete Jack the Ripper'. On reflection it was probably irritation. At that time I was curator of the City of London Police Museum and as part of my duties was constantly meeting people who wanted information on the subject. The Police Museum had very little to offer. Much earlier, as a very young policeman, I had identified and rescued a glass negative of Kelly's room (there was supposed to be a book of photographs) but was thwarted from any further discoveries by the attitudes then commonplace at that time. Several years of exposure to the constant regurgitation of theories and the nonsense that one often hears on such occasions led to a growing irritation with the subject and the thought that an objective book, or at least as objective as I could make it, might scrape away some of this overlay so as to give a better concentration on the facts and the reality of the subject.

It is this objectivity which I have always tried to maintain. My concern has always been that if we continue to add layer after layer of theory upon the known facts that eventually, if we have not done so already, the essential fact or facts that might turn the whole case on its head and give us an answer to the mystery will be either obscured or lost completely.

Something similar had happened to a previous book 'The Houndsditch Murders and the Siege of Sidney Street' (now in Penguin). Some years earlier I had salvaged from the waste paper sacks and the shredding machines the complete investigative records relating to the murder of three City of London policemen in 1910. I had the original handwritten statements as well as the typed copies. I suspect that I was the only person who had ever read the complete record of original papers and copies. In spite of a number of arrests and a trial at the Old Bailey nobody was ever convicted of these murders although the necessary evidence to identify the man who fired the fatal shots was there in the originals. What had happened was that as the papers had made their way up through the system the key facts, unimportant in themselves but damning when brought together, had been deleted from the typed copies when the papers had been 'tidied' up by successive hands to make a prosecution case.

In the same way this is a danger that I feel whenever each new theory comes along. Few new facts, or none at all, a lot of theorising and a possible further obscuration of the minutiae which just might solve this case.

It is not that I am not tempted by theories. I came perilously close to theorising once myself by suggesting the name of Timothy Donovan, the lodging house keeper who gave evidence at the Chapman inquest. But it was a theory that never got started because he died one week before the Kelly killing. Or at least I thought he did. Others have now suggested that he might have been the Timothy Donovan who was repeatedly charged with assaults in 1887 and 1888 and eventually indicted for murdering his wife in 1904. There is no evidence either way that one or other is the same Donovan who gave evidence at the Chapman inquest. Interestingly, however, both of them make a fairly close match to the FBI psychological Profile of the Ripper - a male in his late twenties, local resident, in trouble with the police before (Donovan Two and possibly Donovan the lodging house keeper as such keepers tended to be ticket-of-leave men).

Somebody such as a Timothy Donovan is, in my opinion, far more likely to have been Jack the Ripper than Druitt, Clarence, Maybrick et al, anyone of whom could win a fortune in libel actions if they were alive today.

The reality, I am sure, is someone like Donovan, someone quite commonplace, semi-literate, living and working locally, and known to most of the victims; someone who, after each of the murders, would stand in the crowd, enjoying the spectacle, hugging himself inwardly and thinking "I did all this"

Donald Rumbelow is a freelance writer and lecturer whose books include The Complete Jack the Ripper (Original publication W.H. Allen, 1975. Revised editions W.H. Allen (1988) and Penguin Books Ltd.)

Neal Shelden
JTR Enthusiast

JACK THE RIPPER WAS A 'LOCAL'

On 30th September 1888, he murdered Elizabeth Stride at Berner Street, then west to Mitre Square within the City boundary and murdered Catherine Eddowes. Hurried back east, stopping briefly at Goulsten Street but clearly heading for home somewhere in Spitalfields or Whitechapel. He was seen in the company of both women by two separate witnesses 'Israel Schwartz' and 'Joseph Lawende', who described him as aged about thirty, with a moustache, and wearing working class clothes.

At 108 - 119 Wentworth Model Dwellings, Goulsten Street, he dropped a portion of Catherine Eddowes' bloodstained apron and wrote in chalk on the wall 'The Juwes are the men that will not be blamed for nothing'. The wording appears to reveal the author as an anti-semitic gentile, and the racial insult of 'LIPSKI!' used at Berner Street, adds to the credibility of that hypothesis. However, the double meaning of the words could also be interpreted as a Jew expressing contempt for his own community that for some reason or other, treated him as an outcast.

He was probably unemployed for a prolonged period leading up to the crimes. Stole from his victims, brass rings from Annie Chapman and money from Elizabeth Stride. But robbery was not the motive. The feeling of self-worthlessness in a man of only average ability was made irreversible by his occasional use of local prostitutes that caused him either to become infected with a sexually transmitted disease, or a victim of a prostitute's con-trick.

The deadly cocktail of humiliation compelled him to attack prostitutes prior to the autumn of 1888 but he was never arrested for those crimes, and in consequence the ferocity of the crime increased up to the complete destruction of Mary Kelly.

Medical evidence at the time tends to indicate a right-handed killer, without medical skill.

CONCLUSION: Jack the Ripper was possibly arrested and imprisoned for a lesser offence after 9th November 1888 and the police were completely unaware they had caught him. His state of mind deteriorated in prison and he was either sent directly to an asylum, or released into the care of his family or friends, and they eventually placed him in an asylum, where it is likely he died.

The cowardly miscreant remains unnamed.

True Detective. January 1989 issue. 'Victims of Jack the Ripper'.

N.P. Warren's Ripperana Quarterly Journal No.6. October 1993. Letter concerning poisoner and alleged Jack the Ripper suspect Severin Klosowski (alias George Chapman).

Iain Sinclair
Noted author and expert on London's East End

UNNAMING THE NAMELESS

The names and histories of the five wretched victims of the sociopathic serial killer known as "Jack the Ripper" are clearly documented: death certificates, coroners' reports, mortuary portraits, places of burial. And yet, despite uncatalogued libraries of research and speculation, the identity (or identities) of the murderer remains elusive. This, it seems to me, is as it should be. Triumphalist investigators, in announcing the latest "solution", merely parade some avatar of their own devising to stand in the place of a necessary absence. They should not be allowed to succeed. The re-naming of Jack would also be a kind of rebirth, a final obscenity.

Aleister Crowley, in a typically feline essay (Cambridge, 1988), proposes that the topography of the Whitechapel murders spells out a magical formula, conferring "the gift of invisibility" on the initiate responsible for directing the slaughter. The assassin's curse would then be to remain forever present, unseen by those who search for him. Jack is so much *there* that he merges with the stones, the moss, the grid of future streets. His immortality consists in his being unknown, remembered for what he never was. While we persist in thinking of him, he cannot escape. We assign spectral boundaries to that which is inevitably shapeless. As new names are added to the list of infamy, so is Jack's signature scribbled over, erased.

Whether or not the bodies of the victims were laid out "to describe the averse pentagram", I do not know. That a malign presence continues to haunt the territory is not to be doubted: the presënce of the Ripperologist, the memory slave. This business of sifting evidence and nominating a scapegoat is both unnecessary and unwise. It is my perverse contention that the classic English murder mystery (set in that never-never land beloved of heritage television) would be immeasurably improved by the simple act of ripping out the final chapter, the denouement, the naming of the killer - who, thanks to the inventiveness of his crime, is already the co-author of the tale. I have a weakness for the *Murder on the Orient Express* solution: all guilty! A paranoid take on the most paranoid of events. The Druitts, Clarences, Stephensons, Gulls - all in it, all implicated. Victorian males with bad haircuts, reprehensible moustaches and beards. The books that accuse them should be treated like the fictions they are, judged for their narrative richness, the depth of the characterisations. Stephen Knight's now discredited *Final Solution* with its cast of Masonic conspirators (surgeon, coachman, painter) reads like the script of a play that Strindberg rejected as over the top.

The most extreme of Whitechapel's psychic dowsers is John Morrison, author of the "typed and photostated" *Jimmy Kelly's Year of the Ripper Murders.* Morrison (interviewed for BBC's *The Late Show)* spoke of being able to travel backwards down the thread of time in order to interrogate Marie Jeanette Kelly. He warned the film crew: "If I could go back, if all your cameramen and crew could go back, to see pretty Mary Kelly and share a drink with her in the Britannia, we'd never let her be murdered. But once you stop the murder, you can forget the BBC. We could never come back. We'd be stopped in time". Fixed in that treacherous mirror-lens where killer and detective meet and mingle. All those who keep the pain alive by describing its parameters. The truly guilty men, the writers.

A short bibliography of books with some element of the Whitechapel Murders.

Muscat's Würm. Albion Village Press, 1972. Poems. Illustrated by 'William Gull'.

The Birth Rug. Albion Village Press, 1973. Poems.

Lud Heat. Albion Village Press, 1975. Poems & Speculative Essays.

Suicide Bridge. Albion Village Press, 1979. Poems & Speculative Essays.

White Chappell, Scarlet Tracings. Goldmark, 1987. Fiction.

Downriver (or, The Vessels of Wrath). Paladin, 1991. Fiction.

Radon Daughters. Jonathan Cape, 1994. Fiction.

Christopher S. Smith
JTR Enthusiast

JACK THE RIPPER AND: THE ALEMBIC CONNECTION

MY CURIOSITY INTO THE Whitechapel, Jack the Ripper murders intensified after discovering the formation of the Hermetic Order Of The Golden Dawn, by one, Doctor William Wynn Westcott, in the very year the murders occurred.

Certain members of this group were influenced into believing that the uterus organ of a female was aligned to what was known as the alembic, that being the equipment that was used to produce gold from base metals in ancient alchemist days.

Doctor Westcott was a London surgeon, and deputy Coroner of Middlesex at the time, and was a keen occultist.

My interest was further roused by the words as spoken by Coroner Wynn Baxter who presided over the inquest on the body of Annie Chapman on 27th September 1888: "It must have been someone who had considerable anatomical knowledge and skill and someone who frequented a post-mortem room." The only reason for the killing appeared to be for the murderer to possess himself of the uterus and nothing else. "No mere slaughterer of animals could have carried out these operations".

By taking in these words and researching them, the Lancet medical magazine was describing a sub-total abdominal hysterectomy, the first of which was performed in Boston, U.S.A. in 1853, 35 years before the Whitechapel murders were committed.

After studying the Miller's Court murder of the 9th November, I thought at first that this was a blood sacrifice offered after the completion of the desecration of the Christian cross (where the bodies lay formed a cross - Hanbury Street to Berner Street, and Bucks Row to Mitre Square), but after many hours of contemplation, the operation performed negated this. From there on the alembic connection was born.

The work of the alchemist, like many other subjects was changing; sex, politics, religion were all being viewed differently in the 1888 period. The practitioners of alchemy began to realise that the feat was impossible. They began to align human bodily organs to the equipment once used.

The alembic was the uterus. The creative organ matched the creativity of the alembic.

Apart from Kelly (who I believe did not die in Millers Court that day) each prostitute was hit in the face and knocked out before being placed on a disused tomb in St. Mary's graveyard (then not used) situated at the bottom of Osborn Street. There they met their deaths before being placed in the streets afterwards.

This theory may seem as bizarre as the case itself, but it was bizarre and unsolved to this day and as Conan Doyle said, through his detective Sherlock Holmes: "If the answer does not lie with the possible, then it must lie with the improbable".

I have had three articles published in the 'Criminologist' plus a 17 chapter book completed on the case. In September of 1987 I had a full page spread in the local newspaper which was followed up by two more later that year.

Patterson Smith
American Antiquarian Bookseller specialising in True-Crime

JACK THE RIPPER

The murders of Jack the Ripper are of special importance to the literature of crime. Based purely on the quantity of English language books on the subject, the Ripper is arguably one of the most famous criminals in history. His career has not only produced a body of literature which forms a collecting genre unto itself, but it has also provided a gateway for the novice collector attracted to criminal history by the Ripper's notoriety and by the accessibility of the literature surrounding him.

It was not always thus. When I first began dealing in antiquarian books in 1955, only two meaningful Ripper books had been published: Leonard Matters' *Mystery of Jack the Ripper* (1929) and William Stewart's *Jack the Ripper* (1939). Each had long been out of print but neither was avidly sought. Only with the advent of many new Ripper books in subsequent years and the centenary in 1988 did broad collecting interest in the subject coalesce.

To me the saliency of the Ripper as the first notorious serial killer of modern times transcends the mystery of his identity. Indeed, many other murders are more "mysterious" than the Ripper case, wherein the principal unknown is *who* the perpetrator was. Consider the Borden murders of 1892, in which two people were slain under extraordinary circumstances; it poses a puzzle of a higher perplexity: how could *anyone* have accomplished it? Small wonder that the Borden case long fascinated the two great pioneering crime writers, William Roughead and Edmund Pearson, each of whom wrote little or nothing on the Ripper.

Nevertheless, the Ripper case calls out for a solution, and authors attempting to identify the perpetrator have produced dozens of interesting theories. (I'll have to say that those involving the Royal family strike me as preposterous, and are not strengthened by the book of one mendacious proponent which rests on a falsehood concerning the discovery of an old manuscript). Such 'solution literature' has long been a major component of the true-crime genre.

Criminal cases which prompt published solutions fall into three categories: (1) cases involving a perpetrator whose identity has been a longstanding mystery, (2) cases which had a judicial determination which was always clouded with doubt, and (3) cases once considered settled which have been subjected to fresh analysis to reach new (not necessarily correct) conclusions. Jack the Ripper and the Black Dahlia case are examples of the first category, the Borden and Wallace cases are examples of the second category, and the Lindbergh kidnapping and the assassination of President Kennedy are examples of the third.

Novel solutions to old crimes have a natural appeal to a curious public, and many engaging works have emerged embodying new theories. Some theses, it must be admitted, are based on speculation, blather, or even deceit. Unfortunately the public is vulnerable to nonsensical theories because the popular reviewing media are usually too ill-informed about the cases to perceive the fallacies put forth. One useful purpose served by some Ripper books whose authors are themselves unable to identify the Ripper is to expose the absurdities of others.

What is my solution to the identity of Jack the Ripper? I'm afraid it's hopelessly banal. I believe the Ripper was an otherwise undistinguished psychopath from the lower orders whose name probably never came to the attention of the police. I also believe that the newly published Ripper 'diary' is a fraud. Book collectors can rejoice in these conclusions, for it means that the solution to the mystery of Jack the Ripper continues to elude us, and gives promise of many more books to come.

Patterson Smith is an antiquarian bookseller in Montclair, New Jersey, specialising in crime. He has written and lectured on the collectible literature of criminal history and is publisher of a criminology reprint series.

Prof. Keith Soothill
Prof. of Social Research Lancaster University

UNDERSTANDING THE TENSIONS OF THE NEW MIDDLE CLASS?

The sociologist is in a peculiar position regarding the identity of Jack the Ripper. Like everyone, the curiosity of knowing the identity is, of course, there but the sociologist is perhaps more interested in the phenomenon that Jack has created.

Jane Caputi (1988) has stressed that " the Age of Sex Crime was first blasted into being in London, 1888, with the unprecedented crimes of Jack the Ripper". In brief, she argues "that still anonymous killer essentially invented modern sex crime".

The challenge in developing a theory is whether the crimes of Jack the Ripper were without historical precedent and whether this episode does indeed herald a new era of sexual violation. If so, the clues to identity may be more usefully sought in the society in which he lives rather than the psychopathology of individuals. In fact, serial killing is not new. So, for example, the Baron Gilles de Rais, born in 1404 into one of the greatest fortunes of France, allegedly murdered between 141 and 800 children, mostly boys. However, different social periods produce different kinds of serial killers.

Multiple murderers are not 'insane' but are very much products of their time. It is not by chance that it is unlikely that there were any serial killers active in England in the 1930s and yet in the inter-war period Germany had a dozen cases in which a serial killer claimed over 20 victims (Jenkins, 1988). Indeed, far from being a randomly occurring freakish event, the arrival of a specific kind of multiple murderer is dictated by the specific stresses and alterations in the human community of the time. Elliott Leyton (1986) emphasises that the multiple murderer is in many senses an embodiment of the central themes in his (more rarely, her) civilisation as well as a reflection of that civilisation's critical tensions. He is thus a creature and a creation of his age.

A hundred years ago there were a new set of tensions producing new types of murderers who seemed to be killing for its own sake. In brief, the newly-arrived middle-class professionals particularly featured, perhaps among those with a morbid sensitivity to their class position. So Leyton argues that "the major theme was one in which middle-class functionaries - doctors, teachers, professors, civil servants, who belonged to the class created to serve the new triumphant bourgeoisie - preyed on members of the lower orders, especially prostitutes and housemaids". Jack the Ripper is not, of course, alone for we know already, for example, that Dr Thomas Cream started to poison prostitutes in London in 1891, offering them drinks from his toxic bottle, and sending taunting letters to the police.

For the sociologist the identity of Jack is not nearly so interesting as understanding the tensions of the new middle class which produced this form of homicide. Indeed, the broader societal question which we need to face is why are there more serial killers in one period in history than another. Currently, there is no doubting the interest in serial killing which has certainly become a growth industry (Soothill, 1993).

References:

Caputi, J. (1988) *The Age of Sex Crime.* London: Women's Press.

Jenkins, P. (1988) 'Serial Murder in England 1940-1985,' *Journal of Criminal Justice*, 16: 1-15

Leyton, E. (1986) *Hunting Humans: The Rise of the Modern Multiple Murderer.* Toronto: McClelland & Stewart.

Soothill, K. (1993) 'The Serial Killer Industry,' *The Journal of Forensic Psychiatry*, 4, 2, September, 341-354.

Author: Keith Soothill is Professor of Social Research in the Department of Applied Social Science, Lancaster University. His main academic interests are in criminology and health studies. He has co-authored *Sex Crime in the News* (London: Routledge, 1991) and *Contemporary British Society* (Polity Press, 1994 (2nd edition).

Philip Sugden
Historian, Lecturer and Author

WHO WAS JACK THE RIPPER?

I'm afraid that I have no patience with the bogus Ripperology that has disgraced true crime writing in recent years. The formula has unfortunately become all too familiar. First choose who you want Jack the Ripper to be. Then plunder the books, the newspapers and, if the budget will stretch to it, the Ripper files at the Public Record Office, for facts which can be bullied into investing your fantasy with a veneer of plausibility. If you can't find anything, no matter - invent it.

I'm not saying that there aren't plenty of people out there, specialists and laymen, with a *genuine* interest in the Ripper case. Of course there are. And it was specifically for them that I wrote my *Complete History*. By returning to primary sources, and carefully discriminating between reliable and unreliable evidence, I wanted to produce a text that was dependable to the smallest detail and to correct the numerous errors that have marred previous accounts of the case. This type of groundwork is laborious but it has got to be done before any serious assessment of the main suspects can be made.

Only in the case of Aaron Kosminski, the Polish Jew committed to an asylum in 1891, do the police appear to have procured tangible evidence linking a suspect with any of the murders. Kosminski was identified by a witness, almost certainly Joseph Lawende, about 1890-91. Lawende was the commercial traveller who is believed to have seen Kate Eddowes with a man near Mitre Square about ten minutes before she was found murdered there on 30 September 1888. Unfortunately he only saw the couple fleetingly and within a fortnight of the event was telling the inquest that he would not be able to recognise Kate's companion again. His identification of Kosminski, coming about two years later, is thus unacceptable. Professor Graham Davies, in his recent report to the British Association for the Advancement of Science, also cautions us against the ready acceptance of identification evidence. He points out, for example, that we only recall fragmentary information about a person after a brief encounter and that the accuracy of identifications at identity parades decline steadily over time, recognition rates falling from 65% on testing immediately after the event to only 10% after a year. Kosminski is, besides, an unlikely suspect in some respects. He did not, apparently, possess any anatomical knowledge, and although Sir Melville Macnaghten undoubtedly spoke of him as a man with "strong homicidal tendencies" the medical reports explicitly and repeatedly tell us that he was a harmless patient.

George Chapman, accused by Inspector Abberline in 1903, fits what we know or can reasonably deduce about the Ripper much better. Chapman lived in private lodgings within walking distance of the crimes. He was single and free to absent himself from home at night and, evidently like the Ripper, he was in regular work. He had practical training in surgery. He matches the descriptions of witnesses exceedingly well. He poisoned at least three of his consorts. He had a fascination for weaponry and, as I demonstrated in my book, a proven record of physical violence against women.

But let's be clear about this. None of this makes Chapman Jack the Ripper. It is important to remember that no direct evidence incriminating him in the Whitechapel murders ever came to light. And if Chapman was the Ripper we would have to accept that he eventually abandoned the knife in favour of poison. I wouldn't say that such a dramatic change of modus operandi is unheard of in the annals of serial murder but it is, at the very least, very rare.

In my view Chapman is our best suspect. But he is only the best of a poor bunch. Which is why I would be delighted if some diligent student out there could come up with a more convincing candidate - just so long as his research is marked by honesty, fair dealing and a proper respect for history and historical sources.

Publications on Jack the Ripper: "Puckridge: A Cautionary Tale",

Ripperana, No. 3, January 1993, pp. 55-62;

The Complete History of Jack the Ripper (London: Robinson, 1994).

Brian Tapley
Crime Writer

JACK THE RIPPER

Up to just recently there have been three highly probables: Druitt, Ostrog and Kosminski. And now we have another suspect; I am referring of course to 'The Liverpool Diary'. James Maybrick comes very close to the picture of the 'Ripper' I have carried around for a good few years i.e.: a psychopath, clever, cunning, driven by obscure motive, who regarded the Whitechapel prostitutes as just so much human garbage to be disposed of; someone of position, whose bearing and dress did not arouse suspicion either from the police or the hapless victims; the killings were drug related when viewed in the cold light of day, so pointless, so savage; the goading letters to the press and the police deriding their efforts to capture him, the Liverpool connection ever present.

Now the 'Diary'. It's a rambling disjointed account which in turn almost leads me to believe that a forgery would have been more precise. Only Mary Kelly is mentioned by name of all the victims together with other tantalising snippets of information. In favour of it I would say the initials on the wall above the bed in Mary Kelly's room is one of its strongest statements. They were not spotted for a 100 years - "Left it there for all to see" says the Diary. The door key mystery explained, he locked the door and took it with him. "With the key I did flee....".

James Maybrick, a native of Liverpool - wealthy cotton broker, a frequenter of brothels and an arsenic addict, was poisoned by his American wife Florence in 1889 - six months after the Kelly murder. Shipping obviously played a major part in Maybrick's business life. The fourth murder took place at the rear of 'The Baltic Shipping Exchange'. In Mitre Square in the basement of the Baltic are several bricked-up foot tunnels that were in use several years ago. Could this provide the answer to the 'Thin Air' syndrome always accredited to him.

The speed at which 'The Double Event' was accomplished rather lends itself to the theory that a Hansom cab was used. He had to leave the scene of Elizabeth Stride's murder in great haste to get to Mitre Square, pick up Catherine Eddowes, mutilate her and then make his getaway, all without being seen. A cab must have been used as running between the two locations would have brought unwanted attention. The Goulston St. message on the wall - it does not tally with the writing in the Diary. The gaps between the killings - is it possible Maybrick was out of the country when the hunt was on for him? Clothes - he must have been in a position to be able to afford to throw away the clothes he was wearing at the time of the murders, except in the case of the Mary Kelly killing when he was nude, hence the fire. The letters sent to the press and police contained Americanisms. It was made public recently that there were pedestrian foot tunnels under the East End. The information they gave was rather scant and vague but they are there.

Another piece in the jigsaw? Suspect Kosminski — I do not regard as a plausible candidate. He was as poor as the women victims were and let's face it they would want to be sure of their money before going off with whoever. 'Jack' must have presented himself as a man of means as they went like lambs to the slaughter even when the 'Ripper' scare was at its height.

Suspect Ostrog - he was already known to the police as a thief and confidence trickster. Though he had the medical know-how and carried instruments he would have been afraid of being recognised.

Suspect Druitt - a failed barrister. The man seen leaving Mitre Square shortly before the body was discovered fits him. The detective who was in two minds whether to detain him or not did speak to him and was taken aback by his voice which was unusually high for a man. The description given by George Hutchinson of the man he had last seen with Kelly also comes close to Druitt. But Druitt was playing cricket in Blackheath the morning after the double event - is that possible after a night like that?

I am sure that a solution will be found - a piece of unquestionable evidence will be discovered that will nail the ghost forever. We may already know and can't or won't accept it. The Maybrick coat of arms declares 'Time Reveals All'. Let's hope it's not too long.

J.C.H. Tully
JTR Enthusiast and contributory author

WHO WAS JACK THE RIPPER?

Who was 'Jack the Ripper'? Well let us start with who he was *not*.

Ask The Man on the Clapham omnibus and you will be told, with great certainty, that he was either 'a Royal' or a society doctor and that - this with a nod and a wink - 'the Masons had a lot to do with it'.

The myth of the mad doctor and his black shiny bag was born after the killings of 'Long Liz' Stride; the others came later, from the many competitors in the ever popular pastime of 'Name The Ripper'. Although merely that - myths - the fact remains that they have become folk-lore, together with images of a phantom who flitted around the labyrinths of Spitalfields and Whitechapel resplendent in evening dress, cape and opera-hat. Never mind that he would have been spotted instantly, and probably lynched on the spot, the legend is there and nothing, I fear, will remove it.

Such romanticisms have so clouded the issue that the realities of the murders have almost been forgotten. Little thought is given to the poor women who suffered such ghastly mutilations, nor to the psychology of the kind of man who could carry out such disgusting rummagings amongst their entrails.

The truth of the matter is that the 'Ripper' atrocities were nothing more than a series of sordid murders perpetrated in a particularly sordid area by, almost certainly, the sort of sordid nondescript portrayed in modern psychological profiles. Modern they may be, but there are immutable characteristics of the human condition which render them just as applicable to the creature who was probably the first British serial lust killer as to the scores who have succeeded him.

If 'Jack' *did* fit the pattern - and I am convinced that he did - then, of course, many of the suspects already submitted for consideration are disqualified immediately, and any future candidates must be judged according to *all* the criteria of the profiles. For instance, it will be essential to know something of their childhoods - because serial killers do not spring ready-made into manhood.

Taking the main characteristics from a variety of profiles, we should, to my mind, be looking for a *man* who:

had a disturbed and female-dominated childhood, with an absent or weak father and a mother whose morals were questionable and whom he came to hate;

because of the lack of a stable childhood, felt inferior, had stunted emotions and became a 'loner';

had a strong sexual urge;

appeared quite ordinary and inoffensive;

was unmarried, or whose marriage had not lasted for very long;

at some time in his adult life had been in a situation in which he was sexually frustrated and spent a great deal of time in solitary brooding upon his hatred of women - his mother in particular - and in fantasising upon what he would like to do to them;

was in his mid to late 20s when he committed his first murder;

lived and / or worked in the murder area and carried out his first killing in the proximity of his home or place of work.

It is now extremely unlikely that the *undoubted* identity of 'Jack the Ripper' will ever be known, but the adoption of a more realistic and scientific approach to possible suspects should result in more believable nominations for the title.

J.C.H. Tully has been described as having a phenomenal knowledge of the whole case. Having lectured on the subject and contributed to Peter Underwood's 'Jack the Ripper' in 1987, he is now writing his own book about the murders. Understandably, he is loath to reveal his own suspect at this stage.

Peter Underwood
Noted JTR author

WHO WAS JACK THE RIPPER?

My own feelings and conclusions are Jack the Ripper was probably Joseph Barnett, a cool individual who had lived with Mary Kelly for about two years and who knew the area intimately. He was also acquainted with other East End prostitutes and may have attacked some of them in an attempt to frighten Mary Kelly off the streets, He was the first man police suspected and was one of the few people who knew how to open the bolted door of Mary's dwelling place from the outside. The murdered woman's clothing was found neatly folded beside the bed as though taken off in the ordinary manner so it would appear likely that if anyone was in the room with her when she undressed, it was someone known to her.

Medical evidence strongly suggests she was murdered in a lying down position - again suggesting that she knew her assailant. Barnett had no alibi for the night of the Kelly murder and there is no evidence that he had any alibis for the nights the other prostitutes met their deaths. Even the joke rhyme could well have been written by Barnett; it certainly applied to him: "..not a butcher, not a yid, nor yet a foreign skipper, but I'm your own light-hearted friend - Yours truly, Jack the Ripper". Joseph Barnett was even known as 'Jack'. He answered the description of the prime suspect, he had the motive, the means, the opportunity and he was known to be violent.

I have expounded this theory in my volume: 'Jack the Ripper. One Hundred Years of Mystery' (Blandford 1987) and in television and radio broadcasts including Wire Cable Network, HTV, BBC Southern, Pebble Mill, Woman's Hour, Start the Week, Jimmy Young, Bob Symes Radio 4, Radio London, Pete Murray, Radio Scotland etc., etc.

Shirley Van Eyssen
Author - Just written first JTR book

WILL THE REAL JACK THE RIPPER STAND UP

The only certain fact on which I think most serious Ripperologists would agree, is that there never has been, and never will be, any really indisputable evidence as to Who Dun the Whitechapel Crimes. Given that, and without making any outlandish claims as to new evidence found under the floorboards, I have assembled all the valid documentation in my book 'Catch Me When You Can' to establish that Jack the Ripper was actually the sadistic Canadian, Dr. Thomas Neill Cream, (aka Thomas Neill), hanged 1892 in London for killing prostitutes. Echoes from the past span a century to endorse this view:

FROM ST. JAMES'S GAZETTE, October 21st, 1892

THE WHITECHAPEL MURDERS:	*THE LAMBETH POISONING CASES*
1)The crimes were all committed in the same district.	1)The crimes were all committed in the same district.
2)The victims were all women.	2)The victims were all women.
3)They all belonged to the lowest order of a certain class.	3)They all belonged to the lowest order of a certain class.
4)They were supposed to be the work of a foreigner.	4)Neill was an American.
5)There were certain marked periods between the murders which seemed to point to the murderer taking voyages.	5)Neill travelled backwards and forwards to America.
6)'Jack the Ripper' had a predilection for writing letters about the murders.	6)Neill wrote several letters about the deaths of Clover, Shrivell, Marsh, etc., to various persons.

7)'Jack the Ripper' was described by the only person who has described him, as wearing a slouch hat.

7)Neill wore a slouch hat when arrested.

8)The Whitechapel murders were remarkable for being, unlike all other murders, apparently devoid of any motive.

8)There is really no adequate motive for the Lambeth poisoning cases.

9)The murders were not accompanied by robbery. 'Jack the Ripper' was believed to be a person suffering from a horrible disease.

9)The murders were not accompanied by robbery. Neill was supposed to be suffering from the same disease.

10)'Jack the Ripper' was evidently a very powerful person.

10)Neill was a very powerful person.

The consensus of medical opinion at the time of the Ripper murders was that the killer possessed anatomical skill -- Thomas Cream was a qualified surgeon. However Cream had been arrested for murder in Chicago in 1881 and was supposedly serving a prison sentence during the 1888 Ripper killings. Corruption was rife, though, in Illinois of the eighties -- soon to become the gangland citadel of Al Capone and his like -- and Cream received a major inheritance in 1887 with which he almost certainly bought his way out of jail. Escaping to England he would then have been in a position to commit the Ripper murders the following year -- a fact that the American authorities must have been naturally keen to suppress.

The likelihood of this having occurred is further documented throughout the book, including two photographs of Cream wearing a horseshoe pin, precisely as described by George Hutchinson, considered by the police a reliable eye-witness to the suspected murderer of Mary Jane Kelly in Miller's Court. That Cream possessed and continually displayed such a pin does not of course in itself prove that he was the same man spotted by Hutchinson -- the 'lucky' horseshoe was doubtless a popular form of adornment. However there were surely not many men established as sadists, prostitute killers, qualified surgeons, users of American terminology, (& etc) -- all characterised by the Ripper -- who also wore horseshoe pins!
Will the real Jack the Ripper stand up -- Dr. Thomas Neill Cream!

BRIEF BIOGRAPHY:
This is the first crime book by Shirley van Eyssen. First published aged 15 she has up until recently specialized in children's books, among which titles are 'Flak', 'Out of This World', 'Royal Reflections' and 17 books in the best-selling Splendour Book series of children's classics. She is at present working on another series for the juvenile market, concurrently with an adult historical novel.

Bill Waddell
Ex-Curator of Scotland Yard's Black Museum and author

THE MYSTERY OF JACK THE RIPPER. WHY DOES IT INTRIGUE THE PUBLIC?

The series of five murders which were committed in the Whitechapel area of London between August and November in 1888, have been a source of interest and intrigue for well over a hundred years. It is a crime that has tantalised the minds of crime aficionados all over the world and has made it the subject of a never ending series of articles and books. Many of them have offered both credible and incredible theories in an attempt to identify the murderer. Few have succeeded in providing convincing answers.

These publications have covered every possibility and given birth to more suspects than any one professional detective could, or would care to consider in the course of a modern investigation. As a crime it can certainly lay claim to be the best known felony in the world. Yet what is it that makes it the source of such attraction to generation after generation of crime enthusiasts? Why does it continue to be a focus of attention for both readers and writers?

The reason may lie in the fact that the latter part of the nineteenth century, was a time when the world was developing in many different directions, particularly in the areas of science and technology, not the least of which were new ideas in detecting and solving crime. These new ideas grasped the attention of the public at large and brought with them high expectations of achievement and an expectation of greater things to come. It was natural for the population to expect that a crime with such a high profile as the Ripper murders would end with a result, and with it an exposé of all the latest scientific methods used to achieve the solution.

It never happened. The investigation in modern terms was a disaster, but in fairness one must appreciate that the problems faced by the investigating officers then and their problems now, are vastly different. For all the talk of scientific breakthroughs, little of it was available at grass roots level. There were no fingerprinting procedures in force. There were no scenes of crime techniques. Enquiries were still carried out using methods based more on local knowledge and a gut response to the situation, rather than the careful analysis of clues found at the scene.

Another aspect of the crime which promotes interest in the public mind, is the mental images that the crime produces. Visions of fog swirling around flickering gas street lights. Faceless top hatted figures clutching knives emerging from and vanishing wraithlike into the mist. The sounds of clattering metal rimmed wheels and horses chattering hooves on granite cobbles. All create the popular image of Victorian London. Place a series of violent murders into this scenario, add the element of sex in that all the victims were prostitutes, and a situation of compulsive interest is created.

It is small wonder that the failure to detect the criminal responsible and bring the murderer to book has ensured a school of avid researchers who would greatly enhance their reputation if they discovered and could positively PROVE the identity of the murderer.

Is it possible that there will ever be a positive identification of the murderer? Only if new evidence can be found in the form of provable documentation, until then we can still wait for a new theory to appear in which we can immerse ourselves.

What I can add definitely to the enquiry is that there is no concealed secret identifying the murderer hidden away in the archives of Scotland Yard. They never had sufficient evidence to identify the person responsible and it seems, nor has anyone else.

BILL WADDELL.
Criminologist and Crime Historian.
Curator of New Scotland Yard's Crime Museum (known as the Black Museum) 1981-1993.
Author of the Black Museum Pub 1993.
Author various articles and papers relating to crime.
Consultant for the Series Murder Casebook. Pub 1992.
Consultant for The Ripper Experience London Dungeons.
Presenter of Central's The Black Museum programme.
Consultant and panel member Cosgrave Murders production of Jack the Ripper.
Consultant for numerous Film, TV and Radio productions.

Nick Warren, FRCS
Surgeon and publisher of 'Ripperana'

THE MYSTERY OF JACK THE RIPPER.

The mystery of 'Jack the Ripper' is now permanently insoluble even though we may attempt to get ever closer to the truth. The suspect has eluded us. We shall never be able to interrogate him, to test the extent of his guilty knowledge, or to question his alibi.

It is important to distinguish between candidates suspected by the police at the time (such as Kozminski, Druitt or Ostrog) and those merely advanced by subsequent literary tastes (such as The Duke of Clarence, Lord Randolph Churchill or James Maybrick).

What evidence was the Metropolitan Police able to adduce in 1888? Forensic science, including fingerprint techniques, remained quite unknown. There existed only three avenues for investigation:

(1) That someone would be caught 'red-handed' by the uniformed police, or denounced through 'private information' to the C.I.D. The uniformed police never arrested an authentic suspect under such circumstances. Montague John Druitt was denounced to the C.I.D. by his family, for unknown reasons.

(2) Evidence of identification. The various Macnaghten memoranda (1894) make it quite clear that the Metropolitan C.I.D never believed that a substantive eye-witness existed. No one ever had a clear sight of the murderer, and Sir Robert Anderson's Jewish witness remains entirely problematic. Why else did Macnaghten place, on equal

footing as suspects, the 50-year-old bearded Slav, Michael Ostrog, and the 30 year-old, clean-shaven English barrister, M.J. Druitt?

(3) Circumstantial evidence. Some legal authorities hold that this is the finest evidence of all. It was various 'circs', that made Kozminski such a strong Yard suspect in Macnaghten's view.

Over the last year it has become clear that Scotland Yard suspected another man, largely on the basis of such evidence. He is known as the 'Littlechild Suspect' after the Special Branch detective whose correspondence revealed his name. D.C.I. Littlechild maintained that Sir Robert Anderson (as contemporaneous Head of C.I.D.) "only thought he knew" the identity of Jack the Ripper, a clear statement that Kozminski was identified in error.

Current research supports the view that Littlechild's suspect is the most promising of the Yard's original suspects rediscovered to date.

Molly Whittington-Egan
Noted True Crime author

WHO WAS JACK THE RIPPER?

It was all Dr. Lyttleton Stewart Forbes Winslow's own fault that he was suspected of being Jack the Ripper, and it is somehow typical of the man that he never realized how suspicious his behaviour must have seemed. On an ascending scale of eligibility, he was medically qualified, he was a 'mad doctor', he kept writing letters about the Ripper, and he was always there, flitting with comical moustachioed face about the alleys, and consorting cosily with the prostitutes:

> "Day after day and night after night I spent in the Whitechapel slums. The detectives knew me, the lodging-house keepers knew me, and at last the poor creatures of the streets came to know me."

I cannot accept that he developed a delusion, defined as an incorrigible false belief *of morbid origin,* that G. Wentworth Bell Smith was the true Ripper. An *idée fixe* would be a better diagnosis by far, arising out of his rigid personality. He variously put up the Ripper as an epileptic, as an escaped 'lunatic' (and he believed in the influence of the moon) and as a middle-class homicidal maniac not yet caged. For his time, these were perfectly sound hypotheses. Modern psychological constructs of the serial murderer as a sadistic sexual psychopath would not have been a part of *his* diagnostic lumber-room, and he would have resisted them to his last huff and puff.

Melvin Harris produced the memorable insight that Forbes Winslow, was 'the first of the leading Ripper hunters to become corrupted by the excitement of the chase'. The doctor seems to have altered from 1889 to 1888 the date on a letter to himself purporting to be from the Ripper.

I first became interested in Forbes Winslow, when, with my husband, Richard, I was writing *The Bedside Book of Murder,* and examining the doctor's rather ludicrous involvement in the Dyer baby-farming case of 1896, at which he strove - and failed - to show that Mrs. Dyer was insane. It is difficult to reconcile his gullibility, his lack of insight, his greed for fame, with his attributes as a respected alienist, a paternalistic member of the humane school of psychiatry, always concerned to defend the mentally ill against unfairness in law and society.

My irreverent description of him as "A distinguished, if ever so slightly batty-looking figure", has caused some amusement, but I hope to redress the balance in the full book on Forbes Winslow which I intend to write.

I used to walk the wards of a couple of fine old-fashioned London asylums as a young social worker, and it is true that I am still drawn in my imagination to those corridors with their loping, leptomorphic shadows. It seems to me that I must fill this gap in the Ripper canon. I also feel that all serious murder historians have a duty to make one contribution to Ripperology!

Molly Whittington-Egan, a lawyer, is the author of *Khaki Mischief: The Agra Murder Case.*
She has also written a number of criminological studies in collaboration with her husband, Richard.
Currently working on *Murder on the Bluff: the Carew Poisoning Case.*

Richard Whittington-Egan
Noted True Crime author including JTR

WHO WAS JACK THE RIPPER?

It is edging up to sixty years now since, as a young boy fascinated by the dreads and drolls served up on the delicate blue pulp of the tuppenny weekly *Bullseye,* I went, fugitive from the academic groves of the South Kensington Natural History Museum where my parents believed me innocently immured, trolling in the East End for first-hand reminiscences of the rubric Ripper days of, then, a mere forty-seven ripe autumns back. And, ever since, I have held, as it were, a watching brief on the burgeoning research and proliferating publications encircling convolvulus-like this still obscure paradigm of pioneering serial murder.

The theories and the theorists have come and gone. My own work has been constructive only in the sense that no effective construction can be initiated until the ground has been cleared. *Destructio ad absurdum.* In my *Casebook on Jack the Ripper,* I concentrated mainly on cutting back the dead wood, pruning the convolvuli, prising away the encrustations of legend which, in the course of the decades, had come to form a sort of lichenoid growth, blurring the outlines of the old facts and distorting contemporary clarity.

As the years have gone by, I have seen more and ever unlikelier suspects paraded for the bloodstained laurels, and I have remained as unconvinced of their candidature as I was when, so very long ago, I was presented with Leonard Matters' Dr. Stanley. And I am no royalist - if that means subscribing to the notion that "the highest in the land" were engaging themselves in the sanguineous elimination of some of the lowliest. Neither can I accept the ineffectual Mr. Druitt as the *grand assassin,* nor

Virginia Woolf's cousin James Stephen. No . . . I must reject them every one, old Dr. Barnardo and all. Although, on the lines of 'my father knew Lloyd George', it would be rather splendid to be able to hail James Maybrick as Jim the Knifeman, since he and his wife used from time to time to dine at my grandfather's table. But, regretfully, I do not feel able to say, my grandfather knew Saucy Jack.

Despite the really quite remarkable work done, and being done, by the newer generation of Ripper researchers; despite the extraordinary late harvest of lucky finds, I remain of the opinion that the nominal identity of the Whitechapel murderer endures securely intact.

My theory, if you could call it that, is that even if we were to uncover the name of the individual whom a canny pressman nicknamed so expertly, guaranteeing him in the process bogey-man immortality, it would mean nothing to us. It would, I am sure, be a foreign name - Russian or Polish. It would belong to one of those immigrants to the late nineteenth-century East End, victims of successive xenophobic ukases, who, having fled the pogroms, imported beyond the Pale a pogrom of his own. He would have been a denizen of deep and murkish waters, clouded by an exotic and grotesquely variant sexuality, which, akin to that of that other stout burgher of Psychological-Pressure-Cooker-Land, the sadist, Peter Kürten, depended for its gratification upon a bizarrerie, a *Lustmord,* embracing the slashing exposure of the warm and quivering viscera of a woman in her death throes. He was indeed an emissary of the country of the purblind. As I have somewhere observed before, the heartening message for the next few generations of baffled Ripperphiles is that the Ripper files seem to be, like the categories of negligence, never closed.

Richard Whittington-Egan, described in *The Jack the Ripper A to Z* as 'The doyen of British true-crime writers,' is the author of numerous works on criminology, including *Casebook on Jack the Ripper* (1975).

John Wilding
Noted JTR author

WHO WAS JACK THE RIPPER?

There are clear signs of a cover-up by the authorities during investigations into the crimes of Jack the Ripper. To quote only several examples:-

Israel Schwartz, an Hungarian immigrant, claimed that at 12.45 am he had seen Liz Stride being attacked outside Dutfield's Yard in Berner Street. Schwartz stated that two men were present at the attack. Despite his evidence being taken seriously by the police, the immigrant was not called upon to give evidence at Stride's inquest. Other important witnesses (including Mrs. Fanny Mortimer, a resident of Berner Street) were also ignored.

The inquest into the sensational death of the fifth victim, named as Mary Kelly, was rushed through in one day. Such haste resulted in considerable press comment. The distinguished coroner, Dr. Roderick MacDonald, did not enquire whether any part of the body was missing. There was no attempt to discover the extent of the injuries, and no attempt was made to uncover any details of the weapon which had been used in the attack. Such conduct was illegal; as if to compound this illegality, MacDonald then failed to sign the certificate of findings.

There are many other examples of police intrigue.

But a cover-up by the authorities would only be sanctioned for the very highest in the land.

The Prince of Wales (nicknamed Bertie), later King Edward VII, was a renowned rake. He was famous for affairs with prostitutes as well as with society women.

My researches uncovered the fact that Bertie had, along with several wild friends, rented a flat above a butcher's shop in Watling Street. This merry group had used the flat as a base to dress up as firemen ready to attend any local blazes. This bizarre information is provided by the reliable Sir Richard Holmes, a long-serving librarian at Windsor Castle. (Edward VII, His LIfe and Times, published 1910.)

In 1888, Watling Street was near to prostitutes' soliciting grounds.

It is my contention that the attractive and young Mary Kelly was picked up by one of the rakes and taken to the Watling Street flat. Here she was bedded by the Prince of Wales. This seduction led to Kelly attempting to blackmail the Crown; this blackmail led to the infamous Ripper murders. (Lack of space prevents relating how the other four prostitutes were linked into the plot and why they were killed.)

One of the most puzzling aspects of the Ripper affair has been the actions of Sir Charles Warren, the Metropolitan Police Commissioner. Why, for instance, did Sir Charles rush to the East End of London and personally wash out graffiti, chalked above a piece of a murdered prostitute's apron? This writing could have been vital evidence. I contend that Sir Charles insisted on destroying the message because he knew that it contained an anagram, left by the murderer. (Out of only 46 letters, two names central to the Ripper affair (F.G. Abberline/M.J. Druitt) can be found. I also contend that two letters sent from Liverpool, and suppressed for 39 years, until the death of Sir Charles Warren, also contained vital anagrams.

Jack the Ripper was, in fact, two people, James Kenneth Stephen and Montague John Druitt. I know that they are the killers, because the insane J.K. Stephen left anagrammed messages stating that this was so.

Publications: A horror novel. Seven performed plays. Contributions to BBC Radio One, Overseas Forces Broadcasting Network and Radio Kent. Various newspaper articles.

Roger Wilkes
Noted True-Crime author and freelance journalist

WHO WAS JACK THE RIPPER?

IF you dislike practical jokes, read no further. The Ripper diary, 'unearthed' in 1991 in Liverpool, is a practical joke. Or a hoax. What it simply cannot be is genuine. Sorry, but while the Ripper could have been one of a thousand men, one man he wasn't was James Maybrick. The clue is hidden in the very first page of the 'surviving text', when the writer describes taking 'refreshment at the Poste House' in Liverpool. But in the year 1888, when this entry is supposed to have been written, *there was no Poste House in Liverpool.* There's one there now, it's true, tucked up Cumberland Street, a ginnel linking Dale Street and Victoria Street in the city centre. But it's only been known as the Poste House for the last thirty years or so. Back in 1888, when Jim Maybrick was supposed to be writing up his ripping intentions, the Poste House went under a name that was much more down-to-earth. It was known the length and breadth of Liverpool as The Old MM - the Muck Midden.

It seems an unprepossessing name for a pub. According to legend, at some point in the tavern's distant past some exceedingly fine ale was found buried in barrels in a cellar that had once served as the landlord's midden - or muck heap. Certainly, the place was known as The Muck Midden in December 1887 when the pub was the subject of a lengthy article in the weekly magazine *Liverpool Citizen.* So why, just a few months later, when Maybrick notes in his 'journal' that his glamorous American wife Florence had arranged a 'rondaveau' with Alfred Brierley, does he write of taking refreshment in the Poste House?

At some stage in the pub's history, the rather unsavoury Muck Midden tag was dropped. Certainly since the early 1960s, the place has been known as the Poste House. At least, that was the name on the sign over the door. But I was a regular there myself in the early 1970s, and remember meeting old timers in the bar who still used its earlier Victorian sobriquet. The Poste House as a name was still comparatively new.

But how new? Perhaps the change *had* been made by the time our ripping diarist made his entry in 1888. Sadly not. A clue lies in the name itself, a reference not to any coaching links (the pub stands in a very narrow street, unsuitable as a staging post) but to the now-disused main post office nearby. It is the nearest pub to the post office front door, and at one time was popular with postal workers who drank there at the end of their shift. (It should really have been named the Post House, but someone at the brewery seems to have tagged on an Olde Englishe 'e'.) The fact is that in 1888, there would have been no reason to name the pub either the Poste House *or* Post House for the simple reason that the post office wasn't built until 1899. In 1888, the site was occupied by a foundry.

The first tentative allusion to postal matters in the pub's name is only found in the early 1900s. In 1906, seven years after the opening of the post office, the pub is listed in the Liverpool telephone directory as the New Post Office Hotel. In 1932, an illustration in the *Liverpolitan* magazine shows clearly that the age of the Poste House was still in the future; above the front window of the pub is a large sign proclaiming New Post Office Restaurant, while above the door the letters MM denoting Muck Midden are wrought in iron.

Shortly after the Ripper diary came to light, I made a discovery that, to my mind, nails the matter once and for all. I chanced on a fragile book of sketches of Liverpool streets drawn by the artist Hugh Magenis between 1886 and 1888. Sketch 55 is of Cumberland Street, clearly depicting some half-dozen buildings clustered around the pub at which Jim Maybrick is supposed to have taken refreshment while deciding that '........London it shall be.' No Poste House in sight. Just a simple sign welcoming thirsty Victorians to ... The Old MM. Poste House? Still seventy years away, I'm afraid, awaiting immortality from the pen of a thirsty joker. As Jonathan Goodman observed (of a different case in a different city) : "There's no more brutal murder than the killing of a fine theory with a hard fact".

Footnote: The above was based on work done prior to the Michael Barrett 'confession'.

Roger Wilkes has written three true crime books. His latest, *Blood Relations*, deals with the case of Jeremy Bamber, convicted of murdering five members of his family at White House Farm in Essex in 1985. He is a freelance journalist working chiefly for the BBC

Colin Wilson
Noted author including JTR and True Crime in general

JACK THE RIPPER

I became interested in the Ripper murders as a child, as a result of an article in a volume called *The Fifty Most Amazing Crimes in the Last Hundred Years* on the 'Fiend of East London.' This suggested that the Ripper was 'Dr Stanley' - the candidate of Leonard Matters, MP. Since no one has ever discovered any sign of Stanley's existence, I later came to feel that this can be dismissed as pure invention.

By the time I came to London in 1951, at the age of twenty, I was writing a novel - to be published as *Ritual in the Dark* - based on a series of sex murders in Whitechapel, and I spent many days wandering around the area, where most of the murder sites still existed. (Miller's Court was the only exception.)

After publication of Dan Farson's book - suggesting M. J. Druitt as the Ripper - I concluded that Macnaghten, who suggested it, was so muddled and inaccurate on the subject of Druitt that the theory had to be dismissed. But I felt that a far more likely candidate was Dan Farson's correspondent from Melbourne, who signed himself G.W.B, and who claimed that his father, an alcohlic dung-collector, had told him he was the Ripper. This seemed to me highly likely - I could see no reason why G.W.B. should be lying about it, or why (in that case) his father should have lied.

When Paul Feldman told me in early 1993 of the Diary by Liverpool cotton merchant (and victim of poisoning) James Maybrick, I was excited but dubious - the handwriting didn't look Victorian and the story of the diary's provenance - given to Mike Barrett by a dead friend - sounded unconvincing. What first began to convince me was the lack of evidence against it. There are hundreds of records of Maybrick's purchase of his 'medicine' (arsenic) in the accounts of the Liverpool pharmacist; not one places him in Liverpool when a murder was committed in London.

When the notorious gold watch turned up - with its inscription 'I am Jack', Maybrick's signature, and the initials of the victims, I thought: "Oh no, this has *got* to be a fabrication." Yet the study of the watch under an electron microscope by Turgoose, proved that it was no recent fabrication, and a subsequent electronic analysis has concluded that the scratches are at least 'tens of years old.' Yet the anti-Maybrick school, led by my friends Martin Fido and Melvin Harris, insist that the Diary must be a *post* -1987 forgery. I have to admit that meeting the 'finder' of the watch, Albert Johnson, at the launch of Paul Feldman's video, and being totally convinced by his transparent honesty, fortified my conviction.

When I was in Melbourne in September 1993, someone told me that the Diary had been proved to be a fake, and I groaned 'Oh no!', since I had just completed a book on serial murder, which was about to go to press, and in which I had nailed my pro-Maybrick colours to the mast. When I saw the article about the 'exposure', I heaved a sigh of relief. What it said was that New York handwriting expert Kenneth Rendell had analysed the ink, and concluded that the Diary had been written around 1920, give or take eleven years. Yet since - as the anti-Maybrick school agree - the Diary is either genuine or a post-1987 fabrication, Rendell's analysis was clearly on the side of its genuineness. And can he really tell the difference between ink used in 1888 and ink used in 1909?

I must admit to being deeply suspicious about Mike Barrett's story of how the Diary came into his hands. Yet about the Diary's genuineness I now have only - say - 5% of doubt.

Of course, it *is* conceivable that the Diary is genuine, and that Maybrick was still *not* the Ripper: that it is merely the arsenic-inspired fantasy of a sick and confused mind. But then, if the Diary *is* finally established to be genuine by scientific tests, *this* will be the time to study the internal evidence to decide whether anything contradicts the facts we know.

A. P. Wolf
Pseudo. of JTR author, who wishes to remain anonymous

THE RIP IS ON YOU

Ripper historians inhabit a very dark and murky world. A world where the ripping apart of a woman - until she is no more than several bundles of bloody flesh - is considered a reasonable topic for discussion over coffee where one of the protagonists might cheerfully ask the other: "So you think her breasts were found on the table and not between her legs?"

A dark world stuffed full of the forbidden and hyper-charged with that deadly combination of sex and bodily destruction. After three years in this dark world I had to get out, in fear for my own sanity and in fear of the attractions that such a deadly subject can exercise on a person. But the others, the 'theorists' and the 'Ripper historians' have been there for over twenty years, in some cases even forty years, and they revel in it.

They bathe in the blood of the victims and score hits off one another with their wild theories and lurid details. Pictures, more and more pictures of naked victims ripped apart and propped against dirty walls and the 'historian' is proud to announce that it is his new volume that is featuring this gruesome piece of deadly pornography for the very first time. A slaughtered woman, ripped to pieces but still with legs intact is laid out for us all to see and where her sex was is now a gaping bloody hole and the 'historians' are proud that this is the very first time that their readers have had to feast their eyes on this spectacle of cunningly disguised pornography. One can't help being vitally concerned for the mental welfare of a group of men who spend their entire time delving into the murky world of murder, mutilation and sexual deviance, and worst of all, enjoy it.

Turning the tragic circumstances of a group of poverty stricken women with no other choice than to earn their living by selling their ravaged bodies, plus a very lonely and disturbed young man who really didn't know any better into a carnival of profitable and murderous lust. Basing their alarmist and outrageous theories on one single point: that Jack the Ripper murdered and mutilated his victims for sexual pleasure. He must have done, otherwise there would be nothing to write about.

Sex sells, especially in combination with murder. But the real fact of the matter - fact is an elusive concept in the world of the Ripperologists - is that Jack the Ripper did not have any sort of sexual contact with his victims, alive or dead. The post mortem reports on every single female victim murdered by the Ripper make no mention of any sexual contact, and contrary to what the 'Ripperologists' try to portray as dismal incompetence on the part of the police surgeons of the time these doctors had a surprising grasp of their subject and a surprising knowledge of the deviations of sexual criminals.

This is the point that all historians have missed up till now: Jack the Ripper was not a sexual criminal. In their search for the identity of the Ripper they have ignored the motive and Jack the Ripper is dead but his motive still haunts us today in sad newspaper headlines from all around the world. Jack the Ripper was not a monster. He was a son, he had a father and he had a mother, and he had a motive.

It is the Ripper 'historians' who have created the monster that still walks the streets of Whitechapel and the world today. It is a sad legacy.

A.P. Wolf is the author of 'Jack the Myth' pub. by Hale, 1993. He is also a writer of subjects as diverse as Egyptology, wildlife and crime, as well as fiction.

Simon D. Wood
JTR Enthusiast and contributory author

JACK THE RIPPER

We expect a lot from Jack the Ripper. He must have a good schoolboy hand and a piece of chalk for writing on walls. He must have a dark jocularity and a command of vernacular, both English and American, for writing epistles to the Press. He must have surgical knowledge. He must be an Heir to the British Throne, a mentally unstable barrister, a Jewish slaughter man, a Tsarist secret agent and a barber. She must be a deranged midwife. He must arouse no suspicion. He must have an intimate knowledge of Whitechapel's streets and alleyways. He must be a Liverpool cotton merchant daft enough to leave behind a hand-written diary and the initials of his victims scratched in the back of a watch. He must have split-second timing. Jack must be nimble, Jack must be quick......

In legend, Jack satisfies all these criteria. Yet in truth he satisfies none. Why? Simply because there never was such a person as Jack the Ripper and, despite all our best investigative efforts, never will be.

Certainly, there was the person who cruelly murdered Mary Ann Nichols, Annie Chapman and Catherine Eddowes, a person who either died or was taken into custody in October 1888. Then there was the person who, coincidentally, attacked and killed Elizabeth Stride in Berners Street.

And finally, there was the person or persons unknown who, in an orgy of brutality, butchered an unidentified female in Millers Court.

Five sordid murders, with three (maybe more) very human perpetrators. A far cry from the almost supernatural "Jack the Ripper", a figure society conjured from thin air in an attempt to give shape and form to the incomprehensible and which was later turned to profitable advantage by various vested interests.

Jack sold large quantities of lurid newspapers. At the same time the political left and right were using him to promote social reform on the one hand and anti-Semitism and racism on the other. During the Autumn of Terror the spectre of Jack loomed large, providing a focus for all manner of causes before going on to achieve the legendary status only time can bestow.

Today, in the productivity stakes, Jack the Ripper is small beer compared with the likes of Ted Bundy, Jeffrey Dahmer, Denis Nielsen or Peter Sutcliffe. Yet it is to Jack that we defer when talking of these killers.

Bundy, Dahmer, Nielsen and Sutcliffe have been revealed as sad, pathetic, sick human beings who between them have not advanced our knowledge of human understanding one jot. They are simply not in the same league as Jack the Ripper, the ultimate serial killer, who over the past one hundred years has taught us more about ourselves than we probably wanted to know.

Jack is very real. Make no mistake about that. He is still out there playing his funny little games. But as for putting a name to him.........

You might just as well try to identify the Bogeyman.

SIMON WOOD set the historical record straight regarding the late Stephen Knight's book, 'Jack the Ripper: The Final Solution', a compelling blend of fact and fiction linking the Whitechapel murders with the Duke of Clarence, Walter Sickert and Sir William Gull.
Together with MARTIN FIDO, KEITH SKINNER and PAUL BEGG, SIMON WOOD hosted a weekly Jack the Ripper seminar in Whitechapel, and has appeared on LBC Radio in a late night Jack the Ripper phone-in with DONALD RUMBELOW.

Stephen Wright
American JTR Enthusiast

THE IDENTITY OF JACK THE RIPPER : STILL A MYSTERY

In the East End of London, in the autumn of 1888, five prostitutes were strangled, their throats cut, and their bodies mutilated. The first killing occurred on August 31 and the last on November 9. It was undoubtedly the work of a single killer. As viewed nowadays, we know them to be serial sex crimes.

Why did the person, soon to become known as 'Jack the Ripper,' commit the murders besides the obvious thrill of getting away with them? It is a mistake to view the killer as someone who simply despised whores; it is more likely that he despised all womankind and had grudges against them.

What of the victims? All were driven alcoholics who every night sold their bodies, courting death for the price of drink and flophouse lodgings. The Ripper well knew how to entice them by the offer of (for them) a large sum, coupled with some humorous remarks to put them at ease.

I nonetheless look upon Mr. Ripper as somewhat ordinary, perhaps having a mild manner, but with a hidden ferocious side -- otherwise, how could he have performed his gruesome work with such cunning and dispatch?

Jack the Ripper could have been just about anybody, from a peddler to the counsellor of the realm. This is, of course, indeed true. But the Ripper was not just anybody -- he was *somebody*: an individual with his own personality and occupation, and parents he might reside with. Then again, he might live alone, perhaps separated from his wife.

Dare I, a Ripper expert, confess that I really do not know who Jack the Ripper was? It is still a mystery after all.

Re *The Diary of Jack the Ripper*: No Ripperologist believes the *Diary* to be anything but a hoax, but what of its alleged author, James Maybrick? While generally not considered a Ripper suspect, he was clever and devious enough to have been the harlot killer.

According to the Littlechild letter, written by an inspector from Scotland Yard, and discovered in 1993 by crime historian Stewart Evans of Suffolk, the true suspect was an American with relatives in *Liverpool*, where Maybrick himself lived. Is this merely a coincidence? I understand that the Littlechild document is now being researched; therefore, the Ripper aficionado community may look forward to some exciting news.

Details of publications, etc.: Essay on Jack the Ripper and essay/review on *The Diary of Jack the Ripper* in Mystery Notebook/The Notebook, USA. Two articles on 'The Ripper' in Mean Streets, Australian Crime and Mystery Magazine. Review of *The Diary of Jack the Ripper* to appear in New Mystery, USA. ABC Radio (Australian Broadcasting Corp.) interview in the spring of 1993 on the then newly discovered 'Diary of Jack the Ripper.'

SUGGESTED READING

Abrahamsen, Dr. D. (1992), *Murder and Madness.* Robson Books.
Begg, P. (1988), *Jack the Ripper. The Uncensored Facts.* Robson Books.
Begg / Fido / Skinner, (1991), *The Jack the Ripper A to Z.* Headline.
Cullen, T. (1965), *Autumn of Terror.* Bodley Head.
Fairclough, M. (1991), *The Ripper and The Royals.* Duckworth.
Farson, D. (1972), *Jack the Ripper.* Joseph.
Fido, M. (1987), *The Crimes, Detection and Death of Jack the Ripper.* Weidenfeld and Nicolson.
Fuller, J. (1990), *Sickert and the Ripper Crimes.* Mandrake.
Harris, M. (1987), *Jack the Ripper: The Bloody Truth.* Colombus.
Harris, M. (1989), *The Ripper File.* W.H. Allen.
Harris, M. (1994), *The True Face of Jack the Ripper.* O' Mara Books.
Harrison, P. (1991), *Jack the Ripper. The Mystery Solved.* Hale.
Harrison, S. (1993), *The Diary of Jack the Ripper.* Smith Gryphon.
Howells, M. & Skinner, K. (1987), *The Ripper Legacy.* Sidgwick Collins.
Knight, S. (1976), *Jack the Ripper. The Final Solution.* Harrap.
McCormick, D. (1959), *The Identity of Jack the Ripper.* Jarrolds.
Matters, L. (1928), *The Mystery of Jack the Ripper.* Hutchinson.
Odell, R. (1965), *Jack the Ripper In Fact and Fiction.* Harrap.
Rumbelow, D. (1975), *The Complete Jack the Ripper.* W.H. Allen.
Sugden, P. (1994), *The Complete History of Jack the Ripper.* Robinson Books.
Underwood, P. (1987), *Jack the Ripper. One Hundred Years of Mystery.* Blandford Press.
Wilding, J. (1993), *Jack the Ripper Revealed.* Constable/Volcano.
Whittington- Egan, R. (1975), *A Casebook on Jack the Ripper.* Wildy and Sons.
Wolf, A.P. (1993), *Jack the Myth.* Hale.

Several of the above titles have been Revised and Updated.

HANDWRITING SAMPLES

25 September, the first 'Ripper' signature.

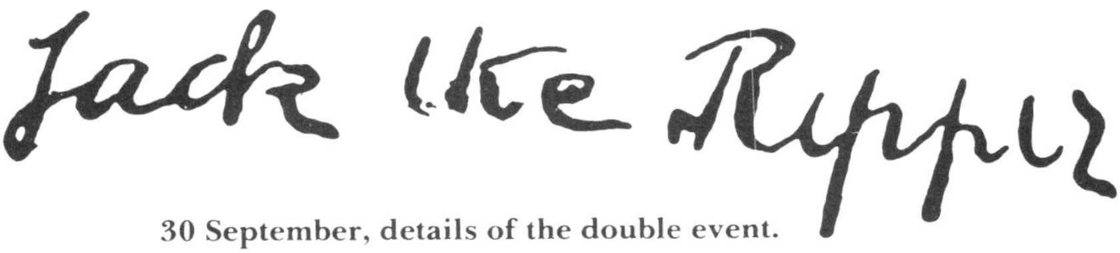

30 September, details of the double event.

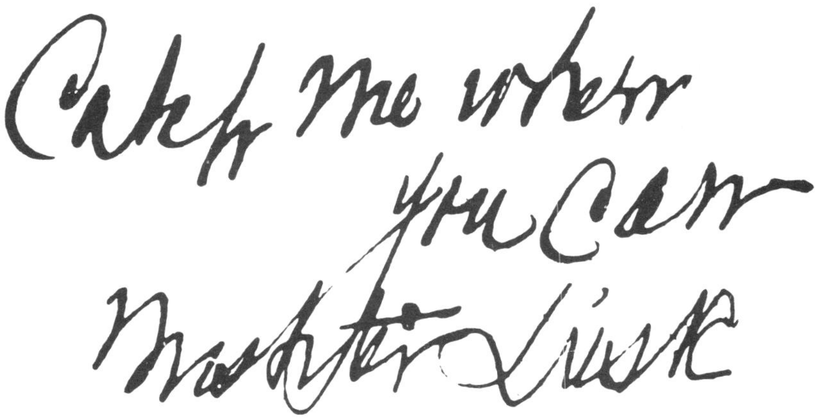

6 October, 'From hell' to Mr Lusk.

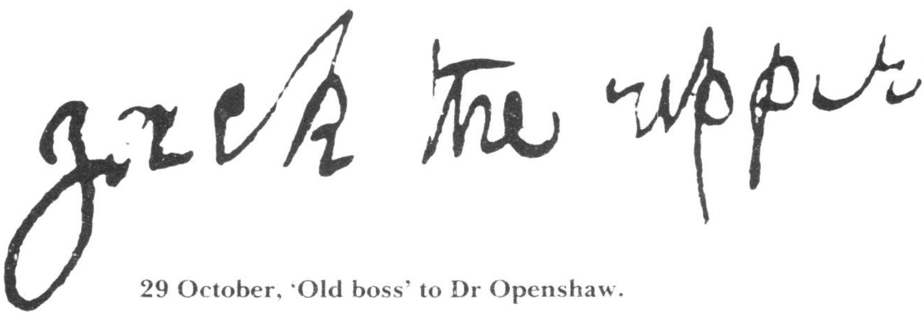

29 October, 'Old boss' to Dr Openshaw.

This book is dedicated to all Jack's victims.....whoever they may be.

Emma Elizabeth Smith

Martha Tabram (aka Turner)

Mary Ann Nichols

Annie Chapman

Elizabeth Stride

Catherine Eddowes

Mary Jane Kelly